SHAPING A CHRISTIAN VISION FOR CANADA

Discussion Papers
On Canada's Future

The Task Force on Canada's Future
Evangelical Fellowship of Canada

Edited by Aileen Van Ginkel

EFC
PUBLICATIONS

Faith Today Publications is the publishing division of the Evangelical Fellowship of Canada.

Scripture references are taken from the Holy Bible, New International Version, © 1973, 1978, 1984 by International Bible Society

Printed and bound in Canada by John Deyell Company

Canadian Cataloguing in Publication Data
Main entry under title:

Shaping a Christian vision for Canada

Includes bibliographical references.
ISBN 0-9695596-1-5

1. Federal government – Canada. 2. Canada – Constitutional law – Amendments. 3. Canada – Politics and government – 1984–   . 4. Canada – Constitutional law – Religious aspects – Christianity. 5. Federal government – Religious aspects – Christianity.   I. Van Ginkel, Aileen, 1957-   . II. Evangelical Fellowship of Canada, Task Force on Canada's Future.

JL65 1992.S53 1992   320.971   C92-093123-5

Faith Today Publications
#1, 175 Riviera Drive
Markham, Ontario, Canada
L3R 5J6

TABLE OF CONTENTS

PREFACE

Will Canada make it into the twenty-first century as a single nation? Will our maps still show us to be in one piece by the year 2000? This question is important to all Canadians, regardless of their feelings on whether or not Quebec should stay within the Confederation.

But are these questions of any special concern to Christians? Will God's purposes be thwarted if the federal government's constitutional proposals are rejected?

The most obvious answer is no. The coming of God's kingdom does not depend on whether or not Canada stays together. But in the here and now, God does call us to be responsible citizens, and as responsible citizens we need to take a stand on constitutional issues.

The fundamental concern for Christians should be *how* Canada should stay together, if it stays together at all. What should be the basis for a constitutional framework within which Canadians can live together?

The basic building blocks for any constitution are the values which all members of the nation hold in common. Too much of the current discussion on the Constitution ignores this dimension, focusing on structural and economic issues instead. In fact, many Canadians fail to realize that the lack of common values is one of the fundamental reasons for our disunity.

Christians have a vital role to play in filling the gap. We can offer to the constitutional process the values that arise out of our understanding of God's Word. Many Canadians who do not accept the basis for our values may nonetheless be convinced of their vital importance to the nation.

Living together as Canadians, despite the deep differences among us, will not be easy. But accepting a common vision for Canada that allows for diversity within unity, seeks justice for the disadvantaged, cares for the environment, nurtures family life, and demonstrates compassion and reconciliation will give all Canadians something to work for together.

The Task Force on Canada's Future, established by the Evangelical Fellowship of Canada in April 1991, has produced a number of papers that deal with shaping a vision for Canada's future. Paul Marshall's paper, "Religion in Canadian Culture," makes the point that religion, particularly Christianity, has played a central role in defining what Canada is all about. If we are to move ahead in understanding who we are as Canadians, writes Marshall, we will have to understand where we have come from in religious terms.

In "Shaping Canadian Values" Don Page writes about the specific attributes that ought to characterize Canada and the Constitution in particular. Attempts at constitution-building will fail if they are not based on an enduring foundation.

Janet Epp Buckingham and Joseph Jolly discuss two central issues in the constitutional drama: Quebec as a distinct society and aboriginal self-government. These are concepts that require much better understanding if we are to succeed in forging a new constitution.

Also crucial to the processes that are shaping our country is the role of the Canadian Charter of Rights and Freedoms. Peter Jervis, a constitutional lawyer with Stikeman, Elliott in Toronto, writes about the need for Christians to understand the

Charter's influence on life and freedoms in Canada.

Christians have the opportunity to become involved both formally and informally in constitutional discussions. Don Page offers suggestions for how Christians can influence the political process.

Digging into God's Word for scriptural guidance and direction in thinking about national issues is a requirement for all Christians. Darrel Reid and Brian Stiller have worked out a series of Bible studies that can be used as outlines for sermons or for group discussion purposes.

Finally, we have appended two resources: the Evangelical Fellowship of Canada's "Submission to the Special Joint Committee on a Renewed Canada" and the Canadian Charter of Rights and Freedoms.

Though the papers in this publication are attributed to individual authors, all members of the Task Force have had a hand in putting them together. Task Force members include Dr. Paul Marshall, professor of political theory at the Institute for Christian Studies, as chairperson; Mrs. Janet Epp Buckingham, Eastern director of Christian Legal Fellowship; Dr. J. Harry Faught, from Central Pentecostal College in Saskatoon; Rev. Joseph Jolly, executive director of Native Evangelical Fellowship; Dr. Don Page, dean at Trinity Western University; Mr. Darrel Reid, Institute of Intergovernmental Relations, Queen's University; Dr. John Stackhouse, professor of religious studies at the University of Manitoba; Rev. Brian Stiller, executive director of the Evangelical Fellowship of Canada; and Dr. William Wan from Ontario Bible College. Mr. Gerald Vandezande, public affairs director with Citizens for Public Justice, and I, co-chair of the EFC's Social Action Commission, were also invited to participate in Task Force meetings.

What it means to be a Christian Canadian will vary with each person who takes the time to think about it. Yet, as members of a community of evangelical Christians, we believe that together we can offer a basis for living in harmony with all Canadians. It is our hope that you will find the articles included in this publication to be helpful resources as you think through for yourself what being a Christian Canadian is all about.

AILEEN VAN GINKEL, EDITOR
November 13, 1991

RELIGION AND CANADIAN CULTURE

Paul Marshall

A. INTRODUCTION

This paper seeks to explore the importance of religion to the development of Canada. We wish to demonstrate that Canada's religions, despite all the faults and injustices of their adherents, lie near to the heart of Canadian identity and to the core of what we are seeking to preserve when we seek to preserve this country.

We will look particularly at the influence of evangelical Christianity, partly to clarify what Canadian evangelicalism is and also to help dispel the notion that evangelicalism in Canada is a stereotyped import of the worst of cultures from the American South. For good and ill, evangelicalism is an integral and formative part of what Canada has been and is today.

We want to urge that as we struggle to deal justly with our differences, we should not marginalize the beliefs that have shaped us, but affirm and build upon what we have received. We will not be able to deal with our disunity and differences, including our religious disunity and differences, in a healthy way if we neglect or trivialize these beliefs; we must acknowledge them honestly and respectfully.

In short, as we take stock as a country, we must also take stock of our religious inheritance.

B. IDENTITY

In a time of constitutional, political, and perhaps cultural crisis it is important to consider our roots. As part of this effort we need to consider the formative role of the Christian religion in shaping Canadian culture. While we ourselves are convinced of the truth of Christianity, we believe that understanding its historical impact is vital for all Canadians, irrespective of their views. Simply put, we believe that Canadian identity must be understood in the context of its history, and this includes its Christian history.

We believe that the roots of our current Canadian malaise go far deeper than the crisis affecting our written Constitution and the structures that uphold it. They affect virtually all aspects of our public life. For this reason, we must look beneath our current problems to their root causes if we are to find creative new solutions. Such values are rooted in our very spiritual being as part of God's creation. This was what Premier John Hamilton Greig had in mind when he told the future Fathers of Confederation at the Charlottetown Conference in 1864:

> When Confederation is carried out we will have a territory which will stretch from the Atlantic to the Pacific. I think that we must all admit that the hand of a greater power than that of ourselves has been directing our labours.[1]

The creative forces that have shaped our nation are rooted in spiritual values that have enabled us to overcome and benefit from the challenges posed by our expansive geography. It was the spirit as well as the brains and the brawn of our predecessors that enabled them to fashion and sustain a nation north of the 49th parallel. Furthermore, without their values our unity would have rested only on the force of law, economic advantage, or geographical barriers, which of themselves are not sufficient for making a sound nation.

Canada's, or rather English Canada's, quest for identity is

proverbial. In contrast, much sentiment in Quebec, and not only among separatists, is secure about francophone identity, but it questions the cultural coherence of anglophone Canada. Many fear that they are, so to speak, wedded to a country with no soul, – a culture that is either vacuous or introverted. Northrop Frye observed that Canada passed "from a pre-national to a post-national phase without ever having become a nation."[2]

Margaret Atwood opined, "If the national mental illness of the United States is megalomania, that of Canada is paranoid schizophrenia."[3] She observed further that the central image of Canada is

> ... *survival,* la survivance, *hanging on, staying alive. Canadians are forever taking the national pulse like doctors at a sickbed; the aim is not to see whether the patient will live well but simply whether he will live at all.*[4]

Sociologists, political scientists, politicians, and bureaucrats poke clumsily at the Canadian invalid to see if the elusive identity can be discerned. Government funds are lavished on this hunt. Historians, philosophers, and especially novelists have tried to discern the shifting contours of Canada's place in the scheme of things. But the patient now seems to lie inert, gazing at American television. The politicians try to arouse it to do battle with separatism, hoping that within Canada, or within the Canadian psyche, lies a guide, a beacon that, if only uncovered, will lead us to a cure.

But what do we mean when we search for an identity? The word *identity* is a recent coinage. It was popularized a few decades ago by the psychologist Erik Erikson and has remained somewhat mysterious ever since. Nobody knows quite what it is. Indeed, we would suggest that a search for identity is necessarily doomed to failure as there is no such thing: no "essence" or "identity" in the sense of a psychological gyroscope within us that shows who we are. Looking for it is a fool's quest. When we look inward (as we should) we may find pains, fears, hopes; we may find a hunger for God. But we will not find *ourselves*. Rather, to find out who we are we must look at ourselves in our relation to what is about us – homes, families, work, friends, environment, language.

Who we are is tied to our life's calling: *calling* means not only a profession or work, but all the God-given responsibilities that each of us has in living with friends, co-workers, fellow citizens, families, neighbours, nature. We are people, nations and countries with specific histories, responsibilities, aptitudes and talents, called to love our neighbours in this place at this time. This is what, if anything, it means to have an identity. In this sense *identity* would best be described as our location in the world and calling in life. Indeed, people and countries seem to search for their identity only when they have lost their sense of place and calling. When a country is dislocated, when it has lost its task and mission in the world, then in order to cope with its alienation it begins a vain inward search for a mythical guide.

Identity, understood as a calling, is closely related to our constitutional order. In practice, the constitution of any country involves the attitudes, opinions, theories, and laws that lie at its foundation and develop, shape, and interact with its fundamental law over time. Hence, most legal theorists agree that in addition to written documents we must include in our understanding of a constitution the interpretations, glosses, and usages that have been developed over time and are understood by consent to have become part of the Constitution. Indeed, any cogent interpretation of the Constitution becomes, to a large degree, part of the Constitution itself. The received opinions, attitudes, and principles not only of the judges but also the population become part of what constitutes us. Therefore, a "constitution" that lacks these ingredients is not properly a constitution. Take, for example, the many "constitutions" developed and promulgated in Europe and Latin America after the First World War. Most did not survive, and some ended in bloodshed. In anything other than the most formal way they were never the foundations of countries. A constitution must be believed in.

This pattern shows in the Constitution even in a narrower, legal sense. The meanings of words, the culture and training of politicians, judges, and lawyers, the opinions of the population, will all shape and reshape the legal order. Our identity, our sense of place and calling, continually shapes our laws and beliefs about law.

C. RELIGION

The widest and most basic dimension of our place and task in the world is a religious one. This is true even for people not conventionally called religious. In the past few hundred years within the secular, rationalized world of the West, religion has often been assumed to be the domain only of certain types of people – *religious* people. Only certain types of activities, like prayer or worship, are considered religious activities. This trend finds articulation in William James's celebrated definition of religion as "the feelings, acts and experience of individual men in their solitude as far as they apprehend themselves to stand in relation to whatever they consider the divine." Such a definition assumes that religion is a leisure-time experience and ignores its cultural and social ramifications.

Though this notion of religion is common in the West, it is by no means universal. It is in fact quite sectarian and bound up with Western culture. It is often used to ghettoize religion. Religion should properly be understood in a much broader way.

In seeking to expand our understanding of religion, we cannot restrict it to questions about God. Indeed, very few of the traditional world religions are monotheistic. Some varieties of Buddhism are in fact atheistic or have no place for distinctions like "theistic" or "atheistic."

Sociologists of religion have frequently pointed out that political movements like fascism or communism, which attempt to articulate an ordered understanding of the whole world, bear all the marks of religion. Indeed, nearly all states and societies seek to understand and express themselves in terms of ultimate meaning. Words like *freedom, democracy* and *human rights*, when considered in any depth, reflect a particular understanding of the nature of human beings and their place in the world. Their meaning, most basically, is religious.

The understanding of religion as that which expresses ultimate meaning is common, even dominant, in modern theology. It is exemplified, for example, in Paul Tillich's characterization of religion as "ultimate concern." It is also reflected in laws which, for example, deal with conscientious objectors who are atheistic or agnostic.

Religion refers to the deepest commitment and deepest identity of a person or group. Hence, the opinion that one may discuss constitutions, politics, education, or sex without any reference to God is as much a religious view as the opinion that we are responsible to God in all we do. An expanded concept of religion allows us to take account of the fact that our lives reflect and are rooted in a particular view of the meaning of life: of the nature of society; of what human beings really are; and of their essential responsibilities, whether to self, society, or another source.[5]

If religion is particularly concerned with the roots of our lives, then we need to pay special attention to its influence on our culture. Indeed, the root of culture *is* religion, in the sense that the basic patterns of our society are shaped by our basic commitment and belief in life which is, in turn, our religion. *Our "god" is that in which we place our faith and trust, and our culture expresses what lies in our heart.*

The religion that has had the major, though certainly not the only, effect in shaping Canada's understanding of its place and mission in the world has been Christianity. It has helped to mold our sense of identity and the pattern of our culture, and has provided many of the assumptions of our constitutional order. We simply cannot understand Canada's identity without some sense of Christianity and its influence.

In emphasizing the importance of religion, especially Christianity, in the development of Canadian culture we are not suggesting that Canadians are currently acting consciously out of an explicit Christian commitment, though it is worth noting that a majority of Canadians still describe themselves as belonging to Christian churches. Nor are we focusing on movements in the past that acted from an explicit religious commitment, though it is also worth noting that this is true for groups as diverse as the followers of Louis Riel, Social Credit, and the CCF. Nor do we mean to focus on the fact that the churches have exerted great influence, though this too is certainly true. Nor are we suggesting that all of this influence has been good or that Christians should have a privileged position and a monopoly over the direction of society. We live in a society with a variety of faiths, and we must deal justly with the realities of a pluralistic society.

What we *are* asserting is the importance of Christianity as a historical ground, a matrix, a world view, a context in which the very meaning of Canada has come to expression. That understanding of Canada, at this important juncture in its political life, means paying due regard to the place of the Christian faith in making us who we are.

D. SOME HISTORICAL OBSERVATIONS ON RELIGION AND CANADIAN IDENTITY

When the United Empire Loyalists immigrated to Canada at the time of the American Revolution, they were not clear about what they had rejected or what they desired. As George Grant put it:

> *It was an inchoate desire to build, in these cold and forbidding regions, a society with a greater sense of*

order and restraint than freedom-loving republicans would allow. It was no better defined than a kind of suspicion that we in Canada could be less lawless and have a greater sense of propriety than the United States.[6]

This produced continuing attempts to contrast Canada with the United States. The perceived advantage of monarchs or governors was that they were above any party, could rule for all, and could be a moral force untainted by partisan interest. In contrast, in the American republic all political offices and policies were tied to a party. One result was the politicization of every governmental office, an evil that was in turn held to be a result of the American infatuation with democracy, an infatuation combined with a lack of authority.

One striking thing about the demands leading up to British North America's Constitutional Act of 1791 is that enlightenment ideologies were not the culture-shaping influences. No one appealed to the democratic doctrines of equality, liberty, inalienable rights and traditions. The elites were anti-republican and anti-democratic; they emphasized order, hierarchy, and paternalistic authority. The mindset was shaped by an (often debased) Christian outlook. The debates of the 1780s produced no Voltaire or Jefferson. They focused not on the nature of a community but on the exercise of particular political authority and on the right of each community (French- and English-speaking) to exist.

One of Britain's responses to the 1837 rebellions in Upper and Lower Canada was to commission a report. The Durham Report recommended that a new political order be founded in Canada. As a result, the British government passed the Act of Union in 1840, uniting Upper and Lower Canada. But while this act introduced a common political order, it did not abolish cultural diversity. The privileges granted to both the English and French communities since 1763 remained in force.

As in earlier years, the response of Canadian leaders was, by and large, to accept the existing cultural diversity as a fundamental fact of political life. They searched for a political unity that was not based on claims of cultural homogeneity or hegemony. They established the principles of accommodation and cooperation as the foundation for public life. Negotiation and compromise, rather than majoritarian views, guided the relationship between the two communities.

The basic assumptions bringing the Fathers of Confederation together illustrate this same compromise and accommodation. The political elites accepted the existence of fundamentally different ways of life. They agreed that the aspirations of individuals, groups, *and* communities must be met within any proposed political framework. They assumed that the rights of nations as well as the rights of individuals would be safe-guarded by the central authority.

Canadian confederation contained, among other things, a treaty between two cultural communities guaranteeing each community the right to its own faith, language, laws, customs, and institutions. In this sense it was a conservative agreement seeking to preserve Canada's religious and cultural heritages. Confederation did not seek to promote human emancipation or progress; rather, it stressed the traditional values of peace, order, and good government. The Fathers of Confederation did not seek to create a new society in a new world; rather, insofar as they thought about it in political terms, they sought to maintain an open society allowing for diverse religious expression and activity.

The appropriation of the word *dominion* for this society at the time of Confederation was not just an incidental biblical reference but was intended to convey a particular spiritual meaning. As William Westfall points out:

> *The Psalmist lifts up his voice in praise of a time*
> *when the true justice of God's commandments will*

triumph over the selfishness and wickedness of men.
It is the just King who "shall have dominion also
from sea to sea and from the river unto the ends of
the earth.[7]

In Westfall's view Canada's motto points to an underlying spiritual theme as well as to a material vision. "The biblical passages," he writes, "foretell a new type of society on the earth when the wilderness of sin and injustice will become the dominion of the Lord."[8]

This religious sense of Canada was continually contrasted with what was thought to be the religion and culture of the United States. Four years before Canadian Confederation D'Arcy McGee summed up this theme:

Where the fault lies aborigine in the American consti-
tutions, ... it is not hard to say. Their authors ... were
so busy looking after their new found liberty that they
forgot that they too could not long govern without
authority. Recusants (sic) against authority they
found it impossible to claim a due portion in the new
constitution for authority. They could not assert the
divine origin of government, the natural right of man
to be governed, the virtue of civil obedience, and all
the other ethical truths, which must every one of them
enter into any human system that ever expects to
merit the blessings of Divine Providence ....[9]

This infatuation with self-assertion was in turn thought to lead to godlessness, corruption, and violence. In 1905 Sir Wilfrid Laurier, Canadian prime minister and Liberal, said during debates in the House of Commons on Canadian schools that:

We live by the side of a nation ... in whose schools for
fear that Christian dogmas in which all do not
believe might be taught, Christian morals are not
taught ... When I observe in this country of ours, a
total absence of lynchings and an almost total

10

*absence of divorces and murders, I thank heaven that
we are living in a country where the young children
of the land are taught Christian morals and Christian
dogmas.*[10]

Beyond these particular criticisms was a general fear of the
American ethos. David Putter summarizes this latter concern in his
conclusion of a survey of Canadian views of the United States:

*Perhaps, fundamentally, what Canadians sensed was
that their culture and their system still largely
accepted the principle of authority, while American
society and the American system did not accept this
principle in any comparable degree ... Canadians
believed that the state, through some authority,
should provide moral direction for the society it governed. Moral direction meant discipline, order,
responsibility, obedience, even inhibition. America,
too, has believed in discipline, order, responsibility,
and the rest, but it has believed in them as self-
imposed, through the acceptance of a Protestant
ethic, not imposed by public authority.*[11]

This stress on order and respect for the community is one of
the principal features that has distinguished us from the United
States. Individual freedom and rights simply have not lain at the
heart of Canada in the way that they have in the republic to the
south.

But this is not the whole story. Canada has not simply been a
submissive hierarchical society. It has also stressed individual
freedom, responsibility, and initiative. Indeed, what may be distinctively Canadian, or English-Canadian, is this balance of
communal order, communal diversity, and individual responsibility.

As recent research is showing, much of this stress on individual responsibility came to the fore in Canada through the influence of evangelical religion. And there is a good case to be made

that the Canadian balance largely reflects the evangelical balance. So it is the place of evangelicalism that we must examine.

E. THE EVANGELICAL IMPULSE
AND CANADIAN HISTORY

To further illustrate our contention that religion has deeply affected Canadian history, we turn to the tradition of evangelical Protestantism. Each region of Canada, with the exception of francophone Quebec (until very recently), has been shaped by the evangelical impulse. In eighteenth-century Nova Scotia, for example, Yankee immigrants from New England felt themselves to be isolated from their counterparts to the south and alienated from the centre of government in Halifax. When political revolution came to the southern colonies, these dislocated and discouraged Maritimers were swept up by spiritual revolution instead. Henry Alline (1748-1784) brought a dazzling message of spiritual rebirth from his native New England, a message that drew Maritimers together in new networks of social cohesion. His message let them articulate their rage at the established authorities and assert their own significance in "acceptable" terms (because they were "religious"), and gave them hope of the life to come amid a dreary life in the present.

Michigan State University professor Gordon Stewart and Queen's University professor George Rawlyk have urged that this "Great Awakening" left a more lasting impression than that, however. The revival undoubtedly functioned as a social activity that provided some immediate and local relief from trying circumstances, but the ideology that emerged from the revival (which glorified "spiritual" Nova Scotia over against the New England that had "abandoned" the faith in an unjustified war) made the Great Awakening a social movement with broader implications. By creating a religious ideology that was specifically geared to conditions in the northern colony, the Great Awakening began to turn the Yankees into Nova Scotians.[12]

Rawlyk has returned to this theme in several writings. He has recently argued that the evangelical tradition, manifested especially by Baptist and Methodist growth in the late eighteenth and nineteenth centuries, constituted the mainstream of Maritime Protestant culture:

> *The political culture of the region ... had congealed by the 1850s into something "fundamentally conservative" and traditional, and this process of congealment owed a great deal to the power of Evangelical religion in this region.*[13]

Indeed, the evangelical tradition complemented these characteristics with its drive toward the reform of society, toward "making it more Christ-like." And Newfoundland, with its distinctive mix of traditions, offers a unique example of the historic and continuing social impact of evangelicalism, as expressed in its various school systems, notably those of the Salvation Army and Pentecostal Assemblies.

This interplay of respect for the traditional faith on the one hand and resistance to and reform of whatever appeared to threaten it on the other affected Ontario culture as well. The growth of Methodism in the early nineteenth century, a movement imported in part from England but especially from the United States, came in the teeth of opposition from the Anglican bishops and government officials. Throughout the first third of the century, the Methodists responded by challenging privileges assumed by the Church of England. Indeed, under the leadership of Egerton Ryerson, the Methodists joined with others to challenge government support of the Church of England, especially through its privileged land holdings. By mid-century the Church of England was effectively disestablished. Now no particular denomination would enjoy official privilege.

The impact of evangelicalism in Ontario went further. Egerton Ryerson, praised for creating Ontario's system of public education, wanted "a common patriotic ground of comprehensiveness and avowed Christian principles." He wrote the text-book, *First Lessons in Christian Morals*, himself.[14] Michael Gauvreau asserts:

> *Public schools and colleges were, however, only the most prominent of a myriad of new social institutions. Temperance societies, public libraries, missionary agencies, public charities, local improvement societies, and municipal institutions such as town councils and police increased in the Province of Canada and the Maritimes between 1840 and 1867. While it would be too much to claim that all of these were created by the evangelical impulse, it is significant that all rested upon the wide acceptance of the principle of individual responsibility that lay at the root of the evangelical anthropology.[15]*

By mid-century, all of the major Protestant churches had been affected by the evangelical emphases on personal and social transformation. In many respects this Christian consensus won important victories, whether in Lord's Day legislation, poverty relief, and so on. The evangelicalism of the "outsiders" became more and more the evangelicalism of the "insiders." As University of Toronto historian John Webster Grant has put it, "in these days ... the term 'evangelical' denoted a belief in the transforming power of faith in Christ to which the great majority of Protestants would have laid claim." Indeed, he continues, "by 1867 church and world were virtually identical in composition."[16]

Although Ryerson and his evangelical colleagues were working for a thoroughly Christian Ontario – whether through the public schools he championed or through the myriad of institutions that sprang up under evangelical auspices, from hospitals and libraries to homes for unwed mothers – their work had farther-reaching effects. McMaster University professor Michael Gauvreau has built on the work of others to suggest that the dis-

14

tinctly Anglo-Canadian *via media* between Tory authoritarianism on the one hand and radical republicanism on the other hand, which was forged in this "evangelical century" (as he calls it), was deeply indebted to precisely this sort of balance in Canadian evangelicalism. Evangelicalism undermined the established Anglican Church and Family Compact in its defence of religious liberty even as it maintained respect for the authority of the Bible and responsibility for all of society. Thus Ryerson, Robert Baldwin, and others conceived the conservative-liberal political philosophy which, it can be argued, has dominated Canadian political life ever since.[17] One can fairly trace the contemporary defense of individual and group "rights and freedoms" back to these crucial advances in Canadian history.

The history of western Canada also demonstrates the effects of the evangelical impulse. William Aberhart (1878-1943) alienated many evangelicals by his eccentric theology and overbearing personality, but his interest in Social Credit seems of a piece with his pastoral concern to help his fellow Albertans during the depression of the 1930s. The party he founded and successfully led went on to dominate Alberta and British Columbia politics for decades. His successor (and the first graduate of his Calgary Bible School), Ernest C. Manning, made his own mark on Alberta as premier. He also contributed to the contemporary political scene by siring Preston Manning, leader of the Reform Party.

Other westerners were moved by the evangelical impulse (particularly in its "Social Gospel" form) to resist oppressive authority and to reform society into a more Christian image. They were among the founders of the Cooperative Commonwealth Federation (CCF) in 1932. Baptist pastor T.C. "Tommy" Douglas (1904-1986), the party's most successful politician, was elected premier of Saskatchewan in 1944 and named the first leader of the New Democratic Party in 1961. Under his leadership, socialized medicine, a Canada-wide pension plan, and other innovations became staples of contemporary Canadian social programs.

In the North, the evangelical impulse led to missions among native Canadians. Anglican, Baptist, Pentecostal, and other varieties of missionaries have brought the message of the Christian faith to aboriginal peoples. The Anglican Church in particular has been active in the North for many decades. The churches brought with them schools, hospitals, training centres, and other institutions.

The missionary encounter with native culture is a complex and painful subject for many. There is no doubt that the record shows examples of cultural chauvinism and insensitivity on the part of the missionaries. The point here, however, is the importance of this encounter, not its goodness or badness, particularly as historians and native leaders themselves disagree over its benefits and damages. What is clear is that most of the aboriginal peoples have embraced Christianity and are vitally concerned to maintain their Christian identity. Very many are committed evangelical Christians. While there is growing interest in traditional aboriginal religions today and a vital movement to re-express the great strength of native culture, it should not be forgotten that the principle aboriginal religion now is Christianity. Aboriginal culture has been and is still shaped by a deep commitment to Jesus Christ. Much of the native renaissance is not a rejection of Christianity but a Christian challenge given by native people to a white culture that has frequently talked more about Christianity than practised it.

Finally, on the contemporary scene, a number of important debates – over abortion, pornography, religious teaching and exercises in public schools, the establishment of private, religious schools (from kindergartens to universities), Sunday shopping, justice for aboriginal peoples, and many other matters – include participants who are motivated by the Christian impulse to honour God and serve one's fellows. These are indications that evangelicalism remains an important motivating force in the lives of many Canadians. They serve as further reminders that Christianity in general has been and continues to be a considerable factor in Canadian life.

These brief historical observations illustrate how the religious shape of Canada, particularly vis-a-vis the United States, has been important to its identity. The idea of Canada having an identity – a sense of calling and an ordered place in the scheme of things – made some sense. As far as Ontario and the Maritimes are concerned, they knew that they were Christian, that they lay in a British tradition and that they were not Americans. This has produced many Canadian myths, some of them true: The hope for "Peace, Order and Good Government" over against the American "Life, Liberty and the Pursuit of Happiness," for example, or our lone Mountie keeping order over against the American "wild west." Our mild manners, our clean cities, our lower murder and crime rates have always been a source of Canadian pride or at least a lessening of its embarrassment.

None of this was or needed to be sustained by a *created* sense of identity. The identity was found in Canada's vocation in a divinely ordered universe. Seymour Martin Lipset maintains that up to the present day the different cultural patterns of Canada and the United States lie in the centuries-old responses of each country to revolution and modernity.[18] Canada's religious traditions, which have uniquely balanced social order with personal initiative and an emphasis on community with respect for individual rights, have provided its sense of place in the world. Our identity has been tied fundamentally to our religion.

F. IMPLICATIONS FOR UNDERSTANDING CANADA

Is this discussion only of historical interest? Is it simply a piece of nostalgia ill-suited to the contemporary world? Is it only a comment on our past or is it also a partial guide to our future?

This has been a conservative discussion, but not in the sense of supporting a conservative political position or simply hankering for the past. It is conservative in the way that Canadians of all political parties, views, and attitudes want to be conservative; it is an attempt to recognize where we, as a country, have come from and hence who we are. One of our vital needs is to be genuinely conservative in the sense of seeking to hold on to something good which is in danger of being lost.

Apart from avoiding this danger, there is also another reason for a proper (and limited) element of respect for our past. No claim to individual rights nor, indeed, any claim to any purportedly universal values or principles is capable by itself of providing a justification for a particular country. For example, any argument for the continued existence of Quebec within Canada might just as easily be an argument which implies that Canada should be part of the United States. For example, a criticism of provincialism and narrow nationalism in a possible Quebec state might also apply to Canada. An appeal to universal and homogeneous rights could justify, in principle, not only a federal Canada but also a federal North America. In short, *no appeal to supposedly universal values, however important, can of itself justify any particular country.* Universal principles can only justify a universal state.

As George Grant said in his introduction to J. and R. Laxer's *The Liberal Idea of Canada*:

> *The statement that the breakup of Canada would be a "crime against the history of humanity" must seem attractive to us at first hearing. But what is stated in the actual words? They imply that "the history of humanity" moves forward to bigger and bigger political units, and that any step away from that movement is a step backward. But if that is a true account of history, why should anybody ever have cared that Canada itself exists and should continue to exist? If*

18

> *"the history of humanity"* calls for ever more com-
> prehensive units, why should we not all welcome the
> integration of Canada into the bigger unity of the
> American empire?[19]

A particular country can be justified only in particular terms –
by pointing to certain desirable features of that country as an
independent state. It needs to be an appeal to history, character,
and idiosyncrasy, not to universals.

Given that Canada's history and identity are tied to its religious history, then any defense of Canada must necessarily contain within itself, either explicitly or implicitly, some appreciation of and defense of that inheritance. If that inheritance is disregarded, then a sense of Canada will be lost, to the detriment of
all its people, whatever their religion. Robertson Davies has suggested that one possible root of the word "religion" is *religare* –
to reconnect.[20] Our present disconnectedness as a country is tied
to our neglect of that connectedness.

G. A PRESENT DANGER

Why then does Canada now look for itself? Why has a sense
of Canada been lost? One basic reason is our gradual orientation
toward the United States, helped in the first place by the economic advantages of trade over a border rather than over an
ocean. Secondly, in more recent years the pervasive impact of
media and especially American media has reshaped Canadian
consciousness. Thirdly, many of Canada's intellectual and ruling
classes have been systematically converted to the ideology of
"liberalism," which we have described as predominant in the
United States. Liberalism in this sense is a type of individualism,
which believes that the goal of politics is to increase individual
freedom. This is now perhaps the dominant view in all of
Canada's main federal parties. It can be detrimental not necessarily to religion in a private sense but to the importance of a
religious heritage in public life. But if Canada's religious tradi-

tions are undercut or driven to the realm of purely private observance, the result will be a rejection of Canada's identity. Hence, such secularism becomes an important factor in our current political malaise.

In an individualistic society (which could not exist in a pure form), people are often taught that their goal in life is self-realization and self-fulfilment; they are taught that ethics are merely "values" (personal choices); they believe that differences between people, such as in religion, are irrelevant and therefore must be ignored in social life. (This is perversely called "respect for religion.")

Some effects of this social situation are well illustrated by Rabbi Dennis Prager in a recent issue of *The Door*:

> *Liberals (whom we have called secularists) are always talking about pluralism, but that is not what they mean. They mean "melting-pot." Pluralism (properly) means that Catholics are Catholics, Jews are Jews, Baptists are Baptists, etc. That's what pluralism means – everyone affirms his values and we all live with civic equality and tolerance. That's my dream. (But) in public school, Jews don't meet Christians. Christians don't meet Hindus. Everybody meets nothing. That is, as I explain to Jews all the time, why their children so easily inter-marry. Jews don't marry Christians. Non-Jewish Jews marry non-Christian Christians. Jews for nothing marry Christians for nothing. They get along great because they both affirm nothing. They have everything in common – nothing. That's not pluralism. But that is exactly what the liberal world wants. They want a bunch of secular universalists with ethnic surnames.[21]*

Pluralism means that different people with different beliefs and different ways of life are living together in the same society. A good form of pluralism is one in which we live together in peace and mutual respect, while acknowledging that our differences are very real and important. But the problem with much current stress on individualism and secularism is that it tries to achieve a kind of peace by denying that the differences exist or that they are important. The result is that committed believers of many religions are told that they must leave their beliefs at the door, confined to private life, if they want to enter public debate. The result is an exclusion of religion masquerading as openness to all. Secularism, in this sense, is a false form of pluralism. By trying to exclude religious considerations from public influence it destroys the very differences it claims to want to protect. It claims not to discriminate but ends up discriminating against any religion that shapes the public life of its members. Where it dominates it negates the life of our religions and our religious traditions.

H. CONCLUSIONS

Constitutions and structures are meant to reflect the fundamental political values of the citizens that are governed by them. When these fundamental values are ignored, rejected, or altered without their input and approval, turmoil and strife will follow. Thus all prospective changes must be evaluated by the degree to which they contribute to strengthening these values in the hearts and minds of our citizens.

As our contemporary political leaders have acknowledged, the values that have often made us the envy of others in the world are rooted in our Judeo-Christian heritage. In 1981 Prime Minister Trudeau reminded Canadians that

> ... the golden thread of faith is woven throughout the history of Canada from its earliest beginnings up to the present time. Faith was more important than commerce in the minds of many of the European explorers and settlers, and over the centuries, as successive waves of people came to this country, many in search

of religious liberty, they brought with them a great wealth and variety of religious traditions and values. Those values have shaped our laws and our lives, and have added enormous strength to the foundation of freedom and justice upon which this country was built ... It was in acknowledgment of that debt that the Parliament of Canada later gave its approval during the Constitutional Debate to the statement that Canada is founded upon principles that recognize the supremacy of God and the rule of law. Faith played a large part in the lives of so many men and women who have created in this land a society which places a high value on commitment, integrity, generosity and, above all, freedom. To pass on that heritage, strong and intact, is a challenge worthy of all of us who are privileged to call ourselves Canadians.[22]

To which the Rt. Hon. Joe Clark added:

I ask that we never forget the faith and the vision of the people who originally brought this country together, the Fathers of Confederation, who from the depths of their own profound faith took as their guide a verse from the Psalms of David, the verse that has since become the motto for our nation: "He shall have dominion also from sea to sea, and from the river to the ends of the earth." We pray that God's sovereignty over our Canada continues to bless and to guide us.[23]

In light of these considerations concerning religion, identity, and our current political problems, we urge that the religious forces that have shaped Canada should be duly recognized in our constitutional discussions. They are not anachronisms that hinder our travel into a plural new world but constitute the very fibre of whom we are as people and as a country. As we seek together to revise our Constitution, we should do so in a way that does not undercut but enhances the place of religion in Canadian society. Our religious values should provide an interpretive framework as we seek to develop and interpret the Constitution, especially the Canadian Charter of Rights and Freedoms. Whatever our religious views or our other differences, as we seek to go forward together as Canadians we should do so in full acknowledgment that the Constitution and Charter are rooted in our religious inheritance.

1. Quoted in Paul Knowles, ed., *Canada: Sharing Our Christian Heritage* (Toronto: Mainroads Productions, 1982), p. 25.

2. Northrop Frye, *Divisions on a Ground: Essays of Canadian Culture* (Toronto: Anansi, 1982), p. 13.

3. Margaret Atwood, *The Journals of Suzannah Moodie: Poems* (Toronto: Oxford University Press, 1970), p. 62.

4. Margaret Atwood, *Survival: A Thematic Guide to Canadian Literature,* quoted in S.M. Lipset, *Continental Divide: The Values of Institutions of the United States and Canada* (Rutledge: New York, 1990), p. 60.

5. See J. Olthuis, "On Worldviews," pp. 27-40, in P. Marshall, S. Griffioen and R. Mouw, eds. *Stained Glass: Worldviews and Social Science* (Lanham, Md.: University Press of America, 1988).

6. George Grant, *Lament for a Nation* (Toronto: Anansi, 1969), pp. 69-79.

7. William Westfall, *Two Worlds: The Protestant Culture of Nineteenth-Century Ontario* (Montreal and Kingston: McGill-Queen's University Press, 1989), p. 4.

8. *Ibid.*

9. D'Arcy McGee, in S.F. Wise and R.C. Brown, eds., *Canada Views the U.S.: Nineteenth-Century Political Attitudes* (University of Washington Press, 1967), p. 120.

10. Wilfrid Laurier, in Wise and Brown, *op. cit.,* p. 118.

11. David Putter, in Wise and Brown, *op. cit.,* pp. 128-129.

12. G. Stewart and G. Rawlyk, *A People Highly Favoured of God: The Nova Scotia Yankees and the American Revolution* (Toronto: MacMillan, 1972), p. 192.

13. G. Rawlyk, *Champions of the Truth: Fundamentalism, Modernism, and the Maritime Baptists* (Montreal and Kingston: McGill-Queen's University Press, 1990), p. 33.

14. William Westfall, *op. cit.,* pp. 6-7.

15. Michael Gauvreau, "Protestantism Transformed: Personal Piety and The Evangelical Social Vision, 1815-1867," pp. 48-97, in G. Rawlyk, ed., *The Canadian Protestant Experience, 1760-1990* (Burlington: Welch, 1990), p. 92.

16. J.W. Grant, *A Profusion of Spires: Religion in Nineteenth-Century Ontario* (Toronto: University of Toronto Press, 1988), pp. ix., 167.

17. Michael Gauvreau, *op. cit.,* pp. 86-92.

18. See S.M. Lipset, *op. cit.,* at chs. 3, 5.

19. G. Grant, in J. Laxer and R. Laxer, *The Liberal Idea of Canada* (Toronto: James Lorimer & Company, 1977), p. ii.

20. Robertson Davies, "Keeping Faith," in *Saturday Night,* January 1987, p. 187.

21. Quoted in *The Door,* no. 114 (November/December, 1990).

22. Global Network Broadcast, "Salute to Canada," June 20, 1981.

23. *Ibid.*

Note: The material in Section E was largely written by Dr. John G. Stackhouse Jr.

Shaping Canadian Values

Don Page

A. WHAT EVANGELICALS HAVE TO OFFER

For enduring and historical reasons, evangelical Christians have a deep concern about the current Canadian malaise. We certainly do not pretend to have all the solutions. But, as representatives of a national institution with experience in reconstruction, we do have a perspective on the problems. We are grateful for the opportunity to contribute to the discussion on the constitutional proposals for the following reasons:

1) A National Perspective

Since evangelicals are to be found in every region and province, every ethnic and racial group from the Atlantic to the Pacific, from our aboriginal people to our most recent immigrants, our perspective is broader than any single region or province. Consequently, we may be able to help resolve the current crisis and unite our nation. Through a lengthy and sometimes painful process, we have begun to learn how to subsume our denominational and regional interests and idiosyncrasies into the greater vision of Christianity based on transcendent values rooted in God's revelation to us as contained in the Bible.

This has been the history of the Evangelical Fellowship of Canada in persuading evangelical communities to work together towards common ends. This movement has been possible because God's truths know no provincial, linguistic, geographical or racial barriers, but have been imbibed by men, women, and children everywhere throughout this age.

For example, those who understand our history and the dynamics of Christianity are not surprised that some of our most effective preachers, such as Reverend Henry Budd and Reverend Ross Maracle in the present day, have been native Canadians. There is also the strong testimony of native Christians such as Chief Billy Diamond, who was recently featured in *Faith Today*, a national magazine published for the evangelical community.

Unfortunately, the secular media have distorted the true picture of aboriginal religion in Canada. As Reverend Joseph Jolly, one of the native leaders on the EFC's General Council, has said, "The media ignore the fact that most Indians are Christians and don't hold to traditional Indian religions; I can be Christian and Indian at the same time."

Evangelical Christianity is well represented among a variety of Canadian ethnic groups. The fastest growing church in Canada today is the Richmond Chinese Alliance Church, followed by other Chinese churches, the Hamilton Vietnamese Church, and the Korean Presbyterian Church in Toronto. In the Vancouver region more than 200 churches, half of which are Asian, have been established among the newer ethnic groups.

Many of our churches are also multicultural. Temple Baptist Church in Montreal is made up of believers from more than thirty different nationalities, including Italians, Chinese, Cambodians, Ghanaians and Arabs. Through their witness, the fundamental moral fibre of our nation is being upheld and passed on to our recent immigrants, because it is rooted in the teaching of a transcendent God rather than in any national or ethnic tradition. We must be poised to build bridges, not barriers, while recognizing our diversities.

2) A Means for National Reconstruction through Confession, Forgiveness, Restitution, and Lasting Reconciliation

We acknowledge that we, along with others, have contributed to the abysmal gap in understanding, appreciation, and acceptance among politically fractious Canadians living in different regional, ethnic, and racial groupings. Too often we have been critical and judgmental. Like others, we found it easier to ignore rather than deal with painful realities. Experience, however, has taught us that unless we first overcome this critical and destructive attitude, we can never expect to work together towards a common vision, whatever our structures might be. Past wrongs and misunderstandings must be confessed; the confession in turn must be received in a spirit of forgiveness, along with appropriate restitution, in order to promote positive reconciliation. We must begin the process and then call upon others to do the same. For if these hurts are left to simmer or are ignored, then we will experience more destructive barricades and flag-burnings as a result of pent-up frustrations and disenchantment with our national leadership.

As in any family or community, cooperative reconciliation is the hallmark of conflict resolution. When the dust had settled after the battle on the Plains of Abraham, the first act of healing took place when the French Roman Catholics offered their churches to the British Protestants for worship.

To this process of reconstruction the nation-wide evangelical community has much to offer. Confession of wrongdoings, forgiveness, restitution, reconciliation, and cooperation are at the very heart of being Christian. To begin the process, we must sincerely and humbly confess to each other and before God our past failings and destructive attitudes. Confession allows genuine repentance, involving a change of heart, to take place. For example, we need to confess that our white ancestors have not always treated our aboriginal brothers and sisters with the respect and dignity that they deserved as part of God's creation.

27

This must not be a superficial generalized confession, but one with specific examples. There are, for instance, the cases of blatantly unchristian conduct on the part of a few who held authority in residential native schools. Only after confession is it possible to ask for forgiveness.

Forgiveness is at the very heart of healthy interpersonal and intercommunity relationships. In fact, it is essential to Canada's well-being. The growing evangelical communities across this land must commit themselves to act as a healing balm for our nation today, just as they have tried to do in the past.

It was under the influence of Christians – a Protestant, Nicholas Sparks, and a Catholic, Daniel O'Connor – that feuding Irish and British labourers found peace in a debauched and riotous Bytown before Confederation. Similarly, the Cree and the Blackfoot Indians settled their differences and resolved to live peacefully in community. We believe that we have something unique to offer in the positive reconciliation of opposing groups that have long-standing antipathy and antagonism towards each other.

Some work has recently been undertaken by evangelicals to effect national appreciation of wrongdoings and the need for forgiveness and reconciliation among linguistic and ethnic groups. This includes the Salute to Canada national television broadcasts from twenty-six cities across our land and Impact 2000 meetings across Canada. Concerts of Prayer, in which confession, forgiveness, and reconciliation were the focus, have been held in several cities. A National Day of Prayer and Reconciliation was held on Parliament Hill for native peoples and church leaders.

Although we cannot turn back the clock, we must try harder to right past wrongs and thereby put an end to the vicious cycle that seeks to destroy us. Restitution was at the heart of the Mosaic law that has been passed down to us (see Exodus 21:18-36 and Matthew 5:23-26). Once appropriate restitution has been made, either voluntarily or through the courts, then through

God's great love for us and the reconciling and healing ministry of Jesus Christ, we are able to extend acceptance and love to all people as the best means to a peaceful and united future. We are, after all, admonished to love our enemies and pray for those who persecute us (Matthew 5:44).

3) A New Cooperative Spirit in our Political Culture

The drafters of the federal government's constitutional proposals have recognized that, though our parliamentary system of government has worked well in Canada, much of the loss of confidence in this system is related to the extremely adversarial nature of our political culture. At its extremes it has produced conflict rather than cooperation. It has accentuated the destructive, power-hungry features of politics and created radical shifts in our political culture. Like others, we question whether that style of politics is most suited to the advancement of a productive and harmonious national community.

We believe that much credibility, respect, and productivity could be restored to our political system if the new structures and processes were designed to promote a more cooperative political climate in which all parties strove for the best solutions in the interest of the community and its citizens rather than solutions designed to produce selfish political gain. This would not be easy. For example, consensus-building rather than political one-upmanship would have to become the object of debate in the House of Commons. Policies would have to be explained and justified in terms of the public good of the community. A wider and more meaningful consultation process involving affected communities would have to be developed. But if we were to set our minds to developing such a system, we have the means for doing so.

Unfortunately, the current public image of our political culture is not conducive to building respect for governments and those who lead them. For example, the Speaker in the House of

Commons allows a style of debate that places political rhetoric above public service. Question Period antics are the most obvious examples of this practice. Governments ought to be encouraged to serve the collective needs of the people in a more responsible and orderly fashion.

Despite the fact that in the last two decades successive federal governments have worked harder at integrating public input into the decision-making process, the public remains disillusioned, steadfastly believing that its input is not wanted or listened to. However, the government alone cannot turn around public attitudes. Organizations such as churches must also work alongside the government to effect a change in our overwhelmingly critical and cynical political attitudes. The new Constitution needs to provide for an ongoing dialogue between governments and their constituents on how public input can be accommodated. Perhaps the system would be similar to the very helpful dialogues that now take place on international human rights, disarmament, and international development assistance policies.

As the Ad Hoc Interfaith Working Group on Canada's Future has reported to the Rt. Hon. Joe Clark, "Integrity of conviction, mutual openness and respect, careful listening and the willingness to be flexible and to work together for shared goals are some of the requirements for this new vision." Participatory democracy must become more than a phrase if we are to construct a positive and responsible political culture in our country. Although we are not experts on the working of our political systems, we believe that we do have enough political experience, particularly through Members of Parliament who share our spiritual convictions and motivations, to make some worthwhile contributions to the transformation of our political culture.

4) A New National Vision for Canada

In a nation of diversities what must unite us is a common national vision. Historically our national vision has been most often defined by what we are not, particularly in contrast to the United States or the homelands of our immigrants. Most recently we have realized that we have lost our sense of direction and purpose as a national entity.

Even as our national existence became less threatened by overt American imperialism, we moved to embrace its liberalism, which emphasized almost exclusively individual freedoms and rights at the expense of communal rights and responsibilities.

Individualism has often been a beneficial force in historical development. But it can emerge in a more extreme form when society is prospering. Individuals tend to think that they are in a position to free themselves from virtually all controls, restrictions, and taboos. Much of this liberation is thought to be good for the individuals involved, but it does not take sufficient account of the aspirations of society as a whole. Such a shift in thinking is rationalized as developing the natural ability, goodness, and freedom of human beings in general, although in fact such attributes are sought only for the advancement of selected social groups, to the detriment of others. In this lie its key failings. This exclusive focus, almost obsession, with extreme individual rights has produced a level of pettiness, selfishness, alienation, frustration, and cynicism that is all too evident in our public meetings and the media. It has also produced unrealistic and competing demands that no government, confederation of provincial governments, constituent assembly, or community of communities can ever hope to satisfy.

Moreover, these demands are superimposed on the inherent and dynamic tensions that make up our country – such as unity versus diversity, symmetrical versus asymmetrical political jurisdictions, urban centres versus hinterlands – and that must also be accommodated in our constitutional debate. As one noted Canadian political scientist has pointed out,

> *Our constitution is now the central arena within which the groups of an increasingly pluralistic soci-*

ety, defined entirely by gender, ethnicity, and language, vie with each other over recognition and acceptance. That competition underlines the descensus in Canada over the criteria to be employed which, in turn, has the effect of making particular constitutional outcomes unstable.[1]

We must focus on what can unite us and not only on what divides us. Within a unified whole it is possible to accommodate the remaining diversities. But overemphasis on protecting and fostering our diversities means that we have denuded our national culture until it has no importance to the institutions and habits of the vast majority of Canadians. In *Mosaic Madness* Canadian sociologist Reginald Bibby has pointed out that if we have nothing in common but our diversity, then we have no basis for a national community. It is no wonder that we have lost our sense of identity and national calling.

We need a new, transforming, compelling, and unifying vision of Canada's future that will be more worth guarding than our lives. It can no longer be a vision based only on our country's bounty, natural beauty, style of government, or multicultural mosaic, but must be based on the principles of what we want to become as a nation. This is what makes the inclusion of a "Canada Clause" in the Constitution so important. When our children and grandchildren look back on this generation, it will not be our affluence, status, or hedonism that will impress them but the quality of our character and action for the benefit of the common good. Therefore, we must be known not only for Inuit sculptures, Mounties, hockey stars, picturesque Rockies, grain-producing prairies, and safe cities, but also for enduring qualities of compassion, peacemaking, respect for proper authority, stewardship, and justice. It is this kind of vision that endures. We Canadians know what we want to have; we need to learn what we want to give and be.

Such a vision will take individual Canadians beyond our narrowly conceived and impatiently promoted self-interest to making decisions for the benefit of the national community. From this individuals will then derive their self-worth. Too often the goals of specific groups are so narrowly conceived that they cause conflict and frustration; there is no overriding vision against which their demands can be evaluated and into which they can be subsumed. It is the business of democratic governments to address and, when possible, accommodate these interests, but governments must also consider the possibility, even likelihood, that not all interests can or ought to be accommodated. Choices must be made among the welter of competing interests so as to focus on overarching values, the pursuit of which all must be committed to for the common good. It is pointless to try to accommodate all opinions in a consensus without a vision.

Our response to technological developments has made us an "instant generation" expecting a quick fix to any problem. This preoccupation with short-term solutions has prevented us from looking at our longer-term interests and values. Now is the time to establish and enshrine these values in our Constitution so that they are at the heart of what we do as a nation. We applaud the drafters of the constitutional proposals for recognizing the importance of identifying enshrinable values in the shaping of our future through a constitutional package. As diverse but united evangelicals, we believe that we have something to contribute to this process of national consciousness-building based on what the drafters have termed a set of "true values" that "allows us to achieve our common goals and objectives while respecting our diversity."

B. OUR POSITION

Our immediate concern is less with the precise nature of the institutional forms that will emerge from the constitutional process than with the establishment of the fundamental principles or values that should underlie and eventually sustain the new Canada. We acknowledge that precise constitutional systems that define the distribution of resources and power are essential to our political and economic functioning, but they are not issues upon which we, as a national evangelical community, are in a position to comment from a distinctly Christian perspective. Many of our individual members, however, have been and will be responding to the invitation to participate in the national dialogue as a means of "building a new consensus for Canada."

We believe that our task, as representatives of the Evangelical Fellowship of Canada, is to help fashion the principles upon which a new political structure can be established and the guidelines for unfolding and interpreting more precisely our constitutional systems. Then we must help reorient Canadian thinking so that we all may have a clearer vision of our future that will embrace, uphold, and promote these enduring values within a new vision for Canada. It is time to do away with the prevailing hypocrisy that values are neutral or relative in a progressive society. We need a clear statement in the Canada Clause of the values that we hold dear as a nation and wish to uphold in all our actions.

Although rooted in our Judeo-Christian heritage, such values and foundational principles are applicable not only to Christians. They apply to the whole body politic of our pluralistic nation of the 1990s because God has made everyone in his image, whether individuals or groups acknowledge that biblical truth or not. Apart from the nature of God's creation and revelation to us, we would have no transcendent values that would be common to all people. It was God who began the process of establishing values by setting a value on creation, by declaring it to be good. Left to their own devices, people naturally incline to construct values for selfish rather than common ends. Therefore, unity of purpose and action can be accomplished only when there is an appeal to higher values. As principles embodying

God's truth for all people seeking to rebuild a national community, these values ought to be submitted to public scrutiny. If, as we believe, they represent the truth, then they are true for everyone and all people. We believe that when given an opportunity to express themselves, people have within themselves a natural desire to acknowledge and follow these true values as a benefit for our common good.

C. RECOMMENDED VALUES TO BE INCLUDED IN THE CANADA CLAUSE

The Canada Clause must be entrenched in the body of the Constitution Act and flow from the explicit recognition in the preamble that Canada is "founded upon principles that recognize the supremacy of God and the rule of law." The values that we believe should be added to the Canada Clause are: respect for proper authority and responsible leadership, responsible citizenship, integrity, caring internationalism, responsible stewardship, compassion, the importance of the family, freedom, justice, and shalom.

1) Respect for Proper Authority and Responsible Leadership

Respect for authority has been most prevalent when those in authority have humbly acknowledged their responsibility before God and humankind for their actions. Such responsibility comes when we acknowledge that supreme authority is vested in God who has established the universe to conform to his will and to function in accordance with his laws. We affirm that "God reigns over the nations" for all time (Psalm 47:8). Thus, every constituted national authority is subordinate to his primary rule and depends on God for its position. As the Hon. Warren Allmand has written:

> *Faith in Christ and the message of the Scriptures have very great significance with respect to public life today. If public life is not conducted according to*

such faith and principles, then it quickly degenerates into an exploitive and manipulative society ... The major disasters throughout history have taken place because Christian thinking and beliefs were not applied in the conduct of political affairs.[2]

Though we believe that leaders should not be above criticism, we are dismayed by the disdain for our political leaders shown by such a large percentage of our fellow citizens. Consequently, their dedication, sacrificial service, and good works are often forgotten and their characters unjustly maligned. When there is no respect for those to whom we have entrusted the responsibility for leadership, we make governance difficult in a free and democratic state. Respect will be earned when the fundamental tenets of good leadership have been recognized and followed.

Leadership must be, and be seen to be, much more than accomplishing public good for private gain. As evangelicals our model for leadership is found in Jesus Christ who sought to serve all men and women without regard to personal distinctives or failings. Rather than self-aggrandizement, Jesus sacrificially sought to enable all whom he touched to achieve their potential in life, as he came to this earth so that each one of us might be able to live life to the fullest.

We are commanded by God to honour, respect, and pray for all those who are in authority over us. We believe that through example and instruction, respect may and must be restored to our leaders who are charged under God's authority to be responsible to those who elected them. In exercising their authority, they should seek to serve their constituents, rather than being served by their office. The greatest example of a serving leader remains Jesus, who came to serve rather than be served.

We must encourage this kind of leadership through education, example, and public recognition. Communities and nations thrive under this kind of respected leadership. For example, in the 1880s Mayor William Howland, a young evangelical Christian, headed a coalition of civic-minded Christians who, with God's help and inspiration, transformed the dispirited, destitute, and corrupt city of Toronto into a purposeful and "good" city.

Without respect for authority, law and order can be maintained only by excessive force. Honourable leadership must be promoted, respected, and publicly acknowledged. To be successful, it must also depend upon the support of like-minded, responsible citizens.

2) Responsible Citizenship

Our institutions must be designed to foster a compassionate spirit that promotes responsible community action. Our national focus must shift from what individuals and groups can get from the government to what they can give, so that governments can carry out more effectively their functions on behalf of all citizens. When we focus on what we can contribute, demands that would produce conflict are subsumed within the larger goal. This can be accomplished without destroying the meaningful diversity of legitimate interests and convictions that would benefit the whole community.

A sense of the whole that is greater than the sum of its parts must be restored. There is a need to realize that what one does locally is important for the nation and vice versa. We must also be responsible not only to our peers but also to those who will inherit our land. We must eradicate the popular notion that we can "have it all," especially since it is often earned on the backs of our children or grandchildren. We must begin to live and make decisions with an eye to the future.

Responsible citizens are responsible not only to their fellow citizens but to God who will, in the end, hold them accountable for their deeds. We have taught the benefits and forms of citizenship but not its values and the importance of these values to the well-being of society.

Responsible citizenship is fostering community by a sense of fellowship. No one is an island unto oneself, but part of an independent whole in which we find our fulfilment. When we have a sense of belonging to and finding our identity and purpose in a common commitment to members of the fellowship or community of believers, we have a better sense of mutually shared responsibilities. For this we need a clearer sense of what it means to be Canadian and a stronger sense of what we are as a community.

We very much appreciate the reference to "the characteristics of each ... community," which is contained in part one of the draft Canada Clause. Too many Canadians seem to find their national identity only by going abroad and experiencing the absence of the Canadian community. Responsible citizens living in a community create their own sense of worth and purpose as an entity. The community spirit must be fostered around values and ideals rather than manufactured in a slogan. Those who promote and exhibit this kind of responsible citizenship need to be publicly acknowledged. They ought to be the real heroes of the rising generation.

3) Integrity

When you lose integrity you have lost everything. We live in a nation that is crying out for integrity in politics, business, community, media, and the church.

Lack of integrity rather than incompetence has been at the heart of the reason that so many politicians have lost their credibility and positions of public trust. In order to have a healthy political culture we must take steps to restore that trust.

We believe that Canadians need to be reassured that our national government intends to conduct its business on the basis of integrity. By including it as a foundational value in the Canada Clause, we can more easily hold leadership accountable to it.

We must then discuss the means of imbedding integrity in the hearts and minds of our leaders and society in general. Conflict of interest guidelines, ethical codes, and codes of conduct have been developed in recent years, but we need to go beyond these in establishing a truly national code and a desire to uphold it. We should also institute confession, restitution, forgiveness, and reconciliation to restore those who have fallen in the attempt.

4) Caring Internationalism

It is only when we are strong at home that we will be able to speak effectively with one voice abroad. Although the federal government has been saying it, Canadians have not yet realized the significance to their well-being of the new global economy. We have so much to offer the world, if we would take our international role more seriously. Too many Canadians have never caught the vision of our role in the world, and have therefore deluded themselves into thinking that, as parts, they can prosper despite the cost to the whole. Do we want to so circumscribe our international activities? Would we be better off if, due to a lack of concern beyond ourselves, we were sidelined in the United Nations, marginalized in the Conference on Security and Economic Cooperation in Europe, bereft of negotiating leverage with our trading partners, unable to resist American cultural domination, or unable to contribute to Third World development? We evangelicals think not; we wish Canada to remain a middle power with a heart and conscience in this world.

In an era of narrow economic nationalism, many Canadians have lost sight of the international responsibilities to which they have contributed so much in the past. The growing global economy and advances in international communication of the past few decades have made our responsibility as our brother's keeper all the more apparent.

We have been privileged to have some of the finest international diplomats and statesmen represent Canada abroad. But they are not the only ones who have affected world development. Many non-governmental organizations, especially the churches whose members are the largest per capita givers of assistance, have touched people's lives in needy areas. Christian values have often been at the heart of Canadian efforts to promote harmonious border relations as an example to the world, to act as a generous, sharing, and caring community member in the League of Nations and the United Nations, to provide the cup of cold water to the destitute, to promote a sense of fair play and justice in the resolution of disputes, and to defend human dignity through the advocacy of universal human rights.

We believe that the tradition of serving others needs to be better appreciated at home and continued abroad. Canadians need to be better informed of their achievements in these areas so that we can all share in their pride of accomplishment. People who work for others in needy areas are today's unsung heroes for a generation of youth who have found few noble role models.

5) Responsible Stewardship

Stewardship is a spiritual principle of environmental management that is based on the fact that God has created all things and retains sovereignty over all things. Humanity is responsible for its use of these things, and must account for the quality and results of its management. Thus, God has committed his created things to people for administration and utilization in keeping with his purpose, allowing them to be used for sustenance, spiritual development, the welfare of humanity and the glory of God. As his stewards we must not forget that "From everyone who has been given much, much will be demanded; and from the one who has been entrusted with much, much more will be asked" (Luke 12:48). This principle stands in marked contrast with materialistic, human-centred attitudes that may justify negligence or the exploitive use of nature for the selfish ends of humanity. It is this attitude, which became prevalent during the Industrial Revolution, rather than Christianity which has resulted in resource depletion, pollution, and the desecration of natural beauty, the results of which we now find so abhorrent.

Sustainable development requires responsible stewardship if it is to be effective. Stewardship means becoming aware of the place of nature in God's creation and then determining how to use what is good to bring blessings to humanity, present and future.

Good stewardship, of course, is a fundamental part of responsible citizenship. It applies to all areas of management, the economy, and government. It is a fundamental principle whereby leaders should exercise their leadership. It needs to be a benchmark for decision-making.

6) Compassion

As citizens turn their focus inward, satisfying their narrow community interests above all else, they lose their motivation to serve and care for others, especially those who have suffered from oppression and exploitation. When we made charity and social welfare primarily a responsibility of government, we created a faceless bureaucratic welfare system that made caring a job or business rather than a passion for serving humanity. It is no accident that our most effective care-givers are those with a self-sacrificing spirit of compassion. Our social welfare system has done much to bring about universal, non-discriminatory social services, but it needs to be reconstituted to reflect compassion.

Throughout Canada's history, Christians have been at the forefront of caring for the ill, the dispossessed, and the poor. It was they who began most of our hospitals, for example. One thinks of Jeanne Mance's Hôtel Dieu in Montreal, medical missions such as that of Sir Wilfred Grenfell in Labrador, and social services and training for the poor like those begun by Marguerite Bourgeoys in Montreal and Lena Bompas in Fort Simpson. In the twentieth century missions were established for the transient and homeless in our urban centres, such as Scott Mission and the Fred Victor Mission in Toronto, and many others across Canada. In their loving compassion, they reached out to bewildered immigrants and dispossessed "boat people." Christian service organizations such as World Vision, the Mennonite Central Committee, the Seaman's Mission Society, and the Salvation Army provide the underpinnings of much of social service development in Canada. For example, the building of the Canadian railway system represents a complex story of vision, determination – and exploited labour. But the courage, discipline, and dedication that kept the crews working came not from alcohol but from the purpose to life given by the caring and sacrificial ministry of the Shantymen's Christian Association and others.

If we are to be a whole society, we must demonstrate compassion in a world filled with impersonal technology and selfish philosophies. As the Rt. Hon. John Diefenbaker has reminded us, "The test of any society, founded on Christian principles, is to be seen in its redemption of waste humanity and the re-making of men." Compassion needs to be included in the Canada Clause.

7) Importance of the Family

The health of a society is only as good as its constituent families, the oldest institution known to humankind. The traditional family that includes a father and mother and their children ought to be our primary basis for social development. Unfortunately, many recent legal decisions, tax-saving incentives, and government programs have weakened marriages and family units. For example, certain tax incentives are given to two-parent families in which both parents work outside the home but are denied to two-parent families in which one parent chooses to stay at home to care for their children.

We must make a conscious effort to restore the basic family unit to the primary place that it ought to hold in society. This would require more structures and programs aimed at developing healthier families and dealing with the causes that have led to increasing numbers of dysfunctional families. Instead of removing children from their parents' care, we need to focus on helping families to become the natural care-givers and mutually responsible healers that the family is intended to be. Families should be restored to their proper role as essential providers of nurturing, companionship, individual security, socio-economic well-being, and instructional, cultural, and religious development. Broken families and those hurt by improper family relationships need to be assisted in rebuilding. It was this concern for the well-being of the family that brought such outstanding evangelicals as Nellie McClung into public life. Now known primarily for her efforts at obtaining for women the right to vote, she also worked to make the lawmakers conscious of their neglect of family rights. We need to develop a similar consciousness today. Stable, responsible, and loving family relationships can serve as an important base for a true sense of community in the public sphere.

Although evangelicals have been at the forefront of family counseling and lobbying, and the Evangelical Fellowship of Canada has established a Task Force on the Family, much greater effort is needed from the government in providing the proper climate for healthy family development. Hence, our Constitution must ensure that all rights be interpreted in such a way as to promote the family.

8) Freedom

At the heart of our democratic tradition has been the notion of freedom. Most immigrants came to Canada to find freedom from tyranny or economic deprivation. Canadians must continue to enjoy fundamental freedoms such as the responsible and sensitive exercise of freedom of speech, freedom of assembly, freedom of association, and freedom of religion. It is the guarantee of those fundamental freedoms that enables individuals and communities to develop and prosper in harmony and mutual respect.

We should not see pluralism as a tolerance of all values and voices but as a means of allowing a variety of expressions so that choices can be made to uphold the highest values. For example, in the current debate over business and medical ethics, choices must be made within an agreed-upon hierarchy of values. We therefore support the reference in the constitutional proposals to the need to balance "personal and collective freedom" with "personal and collective responsibility." Freedom without responsibility is a recipe for national disaster.

9) Justice

Because we are all created equal by God, justice requires that all individuals, groups, and organizations have fair and equitable relations with one another. In terms of economic justice, for example, those to whom goods and services are distributed must be legitimately entitled to a fair share of the goods and services being distributed. To treat people equally does not mean treating them identically. Everyone has an equal right to access of goods and services, but the amount that is finally distributed should depend on actual needs.

Another aspect of justice must be addressed. Justice must be redemptive as well as punitive. Our emphasis on rigorous law enforcement and punishment has done much to preserve law and order, but by failing to deal with the root causes of crime, it has usually ignored the equally important redemptive side of justice. In this regard, a new look is required at the limits of the adversarial process in our courts as well as the preoccupation with guilt and imprisonment rather than prevention and restitution. Otherwise our justice system promotes an atmosphere of despair rather than hope for the future.

Christians see justice as rooted in the loving will of God,

which is directed towards the well-being of those whom he has created. From that perspective, we believe that justice should be directed towards the restoration of the offender and the offended. We need a creative rather than destructive justice system. Foremost in this restoration effort has been Prison Fellowship, a ministry of evangelicals to prisoners. A proper justice system should encourage righteous living and the rehabilitation of criminals through restitution to their victims. "Righteousness exalts a nation, but sin is a disgrace to any people" (Proverbs 14:34).

10) Shalom

There is another kind of justice that must also be pursued. It is known by the biblical term, *shalom*. In shalom, the purpose of justice is the prevalence or restoration of an all-encompassing relational harmony in society. shalom does not signify a superficial absence of conflict or disunity, but the very well-being of a community that is characterized by right relationships among individuals and between people and God. The goal of justice must be the restoration of shalom.

Though shalom applies generally to our legal system, it is particularly relevant to Canada's aboriginal peoples, who have experienced an extraordinary amount of crime and incarceration. We must develop a passionate thirst for justice that leads to restoration and reconciliation. Justice should mean making things right, rather than simply settling scores. As people who take the scriptural principles of justice, compassion, fairness, openness, love, and human dignity seriously, we urge that our governments practise these principles in dealing with the native communities. This involves ensuring that both the processes and the decisions are equitable and that native people are treated with respect. We advocate the practice of reconciliation rather than confrontation, through harmonious rather than adversarial relations.

At the scene of 1990's confrontation at Oka, shalom was the focus of a Christ Across the Cultures Conference aimed at reconciliation among natives and non-natives. In the midst of the crisis stood native spokesman Ross Maracle, who declared, "We believe these days of prayer will refocus our attention on God instead of wrongs and injustices committed in the past, because it is only God who can heal our land and unite us once again." To this we would add, let it be so as we work under God's divine inspiration to effect that understanding and healing at the personal level, while at the same time we move toward defining and implementing aboriginal self-government. With the proper encouragement, we believe, aboriginal Christians could play a key role in finding and developing a consensual solution to the current problems.

To those who would question what Christians can say on behalf of aboriginal Canadians we offer the following conclusion from Canadian historian John Webster Grant:

> *There has been a natural tendency, on the one hand, to exaggerate examples of missionary insensitivity and, on the other, to idealize the state of the Indian societies to which the missionaries came. The myth of the noble missionary seeking to reclaim degraded barbarians has been replaced, in many quarters, by the myth of the noble savage spoiled by meddlesome missionaries. A closer examination even of the recent literature of Indian protest, however, turns up a surprising number of exceptions to the general indictment. Missionaries are complimented for their general concern for the Indians, their dogged refusal to accept the general view that Indians were doomed to extinction, their recognition of the urgency of taking action to preserve Indian communities, and their willingness to resist pressures from white society.*[3]

Similarly, we want reconciliation rather than confrontation

with Quebec. While fully affirming Quebec's distinctiveness, we also want to confirm that Quebec is made up of several distinct societies, cultures, and faith and value communities. Every government should always be respectful of the various communities that dwell within its jurisdiction. We do not want a mechanical division aimed at settling past scores, but creative thinking on what can give us the best for a Canada in which we seek shalom. We can still have diversity or distinctiveness within unity as we have denominations within the unity of Christendom, based on allegiance to common higher principles and a transcendent God.

D. CONCLUSION

For far too long we as a nation have been focusing on what divides us and on supposedly newsworthy aberrant behaviour, rather than on what makes for and unites a healthy nation and society. This focus needs to be made a priority in designing the new Canada. As former governor general George Vanier wrote: "Let us be loyal not so much to the traditions of our past as to their spirit, for only thus can our faith be open to the inspiration of the present and directed to the promise of the future."[4]

Let us not forget that a nation's mission is like a garden: it has to be constantly cultivated and watered if it is to flourish under God's sunshine. The spiritual attitude that must underlie each person's and each community's search for a better way of living cannot be ignored; it must be encouraged to flourish in our land.

As representatives of a nation-wide evangelical community, we do not profess to have a great portion of the answers to our current national malaise. But our roots are deeply imbedded in the life of our nation, and we sincerely and humbly want to do our part in helping to build a national community of communities based on essential values that will unite all Canadians from sea to sea. To this end we humbly submit the above as our contribution to the current debate.

1. Allan Cairns, *"Citizens (Outsiders) and Governments (Insiders) in Constitution-Making: The Case of Meech Lake,"* in *Canadian Public Policy* XIV (1988), p. 138.

2. Quoted in Gerald Vandezande, *Christians in the Crisis: Toward Responsible Citizenship* (Toronto: Anglican Book Centre, 1984), p. 155.

3. J.W. Grant, *Moon of Wintertime* (Toronto: University of Toronto Press, 1984), p. 7.

4. Quoted in Paul Knowles, ed., *Canada: Sharing Our Christian Heritage* (Toronto: Mainroads Productions, 1982), p. 125.

QUEBEC AS A DISTINCT SOCIETY

Janet Epp Buckingham

In 1982 Canada adopted its own constitution, based on the British North America Act of 1867, a statute of the British Parliament. The new Constitution included a section entitled the Canadian Charter of Rights and Freedoms. The provincial government of Quebec did not agree to the new Constitution because it believed its distinctive culture, legal system, and majority language would not be protected adequately. Although the constitution already applied in and to Quebec, the federal government began a process in 1987 to provide for Quebec's formal agreement to it. The Meech Lake Accord resulted from these efforts, but it was not approved by all provincial governments within the allotted time. The federal government subsequently appointed the Spicer Commission to give Canadians an opportunity to articulate their vision of Canada's future. Then in September 1991 the federal government introduced a set of new constitutional proposals which it hoped would appeal to all parts of Canada.

Both the Meech Lake Accord and the new federal proposals included a proposal to add a section to the Charter which says that the Charter will be interpreted in light of the "distinct society" existing in Quebec.

Historically Quebec has been recognized as a distinct society within the Canadian mosaic. In 1774 England passed the Quebec Act which allowed the colony to maintain its distinct language, religion, and legal system. In one sense, Confederation came about because Quebec was unhappy with the merger of Upper Canada (Ontario) and Lower Canada (Quebec) in 1840. A federal system was agreed to partly because Quebec realized that it would receive the powers it needed to maintain its distinctiveness. Since 1867 Quebec has been able to maintain one of the most vibrant and distinctive cultures in North America.

Other provinces also have distinctive features in their constitutional packages. Newfoundland, for example, is constitutionally permitted to fund denominational schools, whereas most other provinces do not have the same provision. This does not make our "constitutional agreement" unequal but tries only to recognize that various provinces have different needs based on different histories. In the same way, to recognize Quebec's "distinct society" in the Constitution does not mean that Quebec is better or preferred, merely that its distinctiveness will be taken into account in certain circumstances.

It is important to recognize the place of the "distinct society" clause in the Constitution. The Canadian Charter of Rights and Freedoms was adopted in 1982 to protect the rights of individuals over against the government. Certain interpretation clauses are included to ensure that the interests of some segments of the population are not overwhelmed by this document. An interpretation clause requires that when a particular provision of the Charter is applied, the rights of certain groups must be considered. Among these are protections for aboriginal people and for women, as well as a recognition of Canada's multicultural heritage. The "distinct society" clause is intended to be an additional interpretation clause.

If we are willing to recognize the variety of ethnic groups, women, and natives, surely we can recognize the distinctiveness of Quebec. Quebec constitutes almost one-third of Canada's population, and its history and culture are part of what makes Canada unique.

The definition of "distinct society" which the federal government has proposed is:

> *For the purposes of subsection (1), "distinct society,"*
> *in relation to Quebec, includes:*
> *(a) a French-speaking majority;*
> *(b) a unique culture; and*
> *(c) a civil law tradition.*

This clause outlines the distinctions that exist and are recognized in Canadian law. It should be noted, however, that Quebec comprises an aggregate of cultures and language groups. It is not a single-language or one-culture entity.

The first two clauses of the definition are readily understood by most people, but the "civil law tradition" requires some explanation. Other provinces in Canada have a "common law tradition" derived from British law. This means that legal judgments are determined on the basis of decisions made in similar cases. Even where there are written statutes, the statutes are interpreted on this case-by-case basis. Quebec, however, has a Civil Code derived from France. The Code is comprehensive in that it has a written law to govern every situation. As each case arises, the judge turns to the Code and applies it to the case before the court rather than comparing the present case to previous cases of the same type.

The civil law tradition, then, means that Quebec judges interpret and apply the law differently. It is natural for the courts in Quebec, therefore, to apply the Charter in a slightly different way as well. In the rest of Canada the Charter applies to all government legislation. If this were the case in Quebec, the Charter would be applied to both government and private cases, as the Civil Code is comprehensive in its scope. Thus, for the Charter to be applied equally, it must be applied differently in Quebec. That is, the courts must make a distinction between purely private actions, to which the Charter does not apply, and government actions, to which it does apply.

Quebec is asking for more than the "distinct society" clause, however. The provincial government argues that to maintain Quebec's society it needs to have constitutional powers over such matters as immigration and culture, which are currently under federal jurisdiction. It also wishes to maintain its strong cultural and economic ties with *la Francophonie*, the French equivalent of the British Commonwealth.

Understanding what the distinct society clause means is a first step in thinking about this controversial topic. We need to try to foster better understanding among peoples in Canada so that we can argue our views sensibly. In the case of the distinct society clause, we must ask whether Quebec should be permitted the constitutional powers it seeks to allow it to encourage its own unique language, culture, and laws. What impact, for instance, will this have for the minority cultures within Quebec?

Students of Canadian history know that Confederation has frequently been difficult and challenging. Nova Scotia attempted to separate from the rest of Canada before the turn of the century. The Métis of Saskatchewan formed their own provisional government and attempted independence under Louis Riel. The Newfoundland referendum to join Confederation resulted in a very close vote. Several provinces and many people have not wanted to be a part of Canada at one time or another.

One of Canada's greatest strengths – and weaknesses – is its diversity. Learning how to build unity in this diversity will not be easy. Yet we have a common heritage: Let's work together for Canada's future.

A NATIVE VIEW
OF SELF-GOVERNMENT

Joseph Jolly

I'm a Cree Indian, born in Waskaganish, Quebec and raised in Moose Factory, Ontario. When I was five years old my parents moved to Moose Factory, but they kept their Indian band status with the Waskaganish Reserve. Today both my wife and I are registered members of the Waskaganish Indian Band.

My father was a trapper and hunter all his life. That's how he raised and provided for his family. He has his own trapline even today. And though he no longer depends on trapping for his sole income, it is still an important part of his life. Some of my fondest memories are of the times when our family lived off the land in the bush.

When I was six years old my older brother Allan and I were placed in an Indian residential school in Moose Factory. My father had gone to a residential school himself, and while he didn't want us to go there, he had no choice. Since my parents, being trappers, lived six months of the year in the bush, it was necessary. It was difficult to be separated from our parents for ten months of the year but, like most other things, you get used to it.

Twenty-five years ago there were no secondary schools on many of the northern reserves. It was common for Indian students to leave home and go to the cities to pursue further education. I went to North Bay, Ontario for my high school education, but much to my regret now I dropped out in my second year. My parents didn't want me to quit, but my mind was already made up. I was fortunate to get a job right away, so it didn't look so bad after all. And I finally got a chance to live with my parents without any interruptions.

Alcohol was a problem in our home, as it was for many Indian families. As children we grew up watching our parents drink. It was no surprise that all my brothers and sisters followed in their footsteps. Alcohol was slowly destroying our home life, and it was only a matter of time before things would get worse.

During this difficult period my mother put her faith and trust in the Lord Jesus Christ. Within two years our whole family responded to the gospel message of salvation. This new life in Christ made an enormous difference in our lives. One of the things that the Lord took from our way of life was alcohol.

A year after our marriage my wife Sheila and I moved to Ottawa and I took a course in chef training after which I worked at the Château Laurier Hotel, National Arts Centre, and the Royal Parliamentary Restaurant. Following three years of apprenticeship I finally completed my training. But by this time my life had taken a new direction.

On October 13, 1974, my wife and I became Christian in faith, after which we decided to apply for church ministry. I resigned my job in Ottawa and enrolled at Briercrest Bible College in Caronport, Saskatchewan. After completing studies at Briercrest, Sheila and I joined the Native Evangelical Fellowship of Canada (NEF) as missionaries in April 1980. For the last eleven years now I have held the position of executive director.

As a native Christian I have personal convictions regarding native self-government. We usually hear only the views of secular Indian leaders. In working with native Christian leaders, I have sensed that they, like me, fully support self-government.

The name "Indian" does not apply to all the aboriginal people of Canada. In Canada there are three distinct groups: Indian, Métis, and Inuit.

There are approximately 500,000 Indians. Just over sixty percent of Indians live on reserves and are members of 593 bands. There are fifty-three distinct Indian languages.

The Inuit, numbering about 27,000, live in small communities scattered across the northern regions of Canada. Though they share a common language, they have a half-dozen dialects.

The Métis are a mixed-race people. Some reside in Métis settlements, but most live with the general population. They number about 60,000.

As a whole the native population in Canada comprises many different tribes, each with its own language, culture and customs. Each tribe is distinct from the others.

The word "missionary" is not very popular with the secular Indian leaders because of the negative connotations associated with it from the past. The native study courses which a number of universities offer do not overlook the mistakes the early white missionaries made in cross-cultural ministries. We should not be too hard on the early missionaries, however. We must understand that in their pioneering work they did not understand the issues of cross-cultural communications. Today's missionaries, by learning from past mistakes, have a better understanding of the need to preserve the culture of the native people.

Today in native ministries the goal of most missions is to establish strong indigenous churches. They do that by training native Christians to be the leaders of their own people. Indians reaching Indians is the quickest and most effective way to present the gospel to the native people.

This principle of indigenous missions is similar to principles being advocated in native self-government. Ownership and self-government are just two characteristics of an indigenous church. Elijah Harper, speaking on native self-government, said that the only way for aboriginal people to get back on their feet is to do it for ourselves. The same is true for native ministries.

I admit that it is difficult to explain native self-government simply. The subject is so broad and controversial. However, as I understand native self-government, I fully support the idea. As a leader in the native Christian church I am encouraged when I see my own people take a greater responsibility in helping themselves. Native self-government will help eliminate native people's dependency on governments.

What do aboriginal people mean by self-government? Carol Goar's editorial in the *Toronto Star* is helpful.

> *[Native self-government] includes control over their land and resources, the right to apply their own laws, protect native languages, do their own policing, take over the education of their own children, develop their own health care system, set their own economic priorities and administer their own social programs. And they want to be recognized as a distinct founding people.*[1]

Another word used by native leaders in talking about self-government is sovereignty. This idea has been at the heart of Indian concerns for centuries. We want to exercise control over our lands and people. When the Canadian government entered into treaties with the Indians, they proceeded on a nation-to-nation basis. What native leaders want now is to have native sovereignty recognized in the Constitution.

Indians argue that sovereignty is not that which comes to them by government decree, but that it is a gift from the Creator. We as Indians believe our right to sovereignty has never been surrendered in any of our treaties.

Even though certain historical documents recognize the inherent rights of native peoples, federal and provincial governments throughout most of the twentieth century have refused to recognize Indian sovereignty.

This is changing, however. In 1985 the Supreme Court of

Canada ruled in the Musqueim case that Indian sovereignty and rights exist independently from the Crown.[2]

The native political leaders' persistent stand on native self-government has begun to pay off. The Canadian public is now more supportive of the native people's cause for self-government. The federal and provincial governments are beginning to rethink their position. In fact, in August 1991 the Ontario government acknowledged the native people's right to self-government.

There is some disagreement among native groups on how to implement self-government, but they agree that what they are seeking is a third order of government within confederation. This would allow them to have direct control over areas such as culture, language, religion, and education, as well as administrative jurisdiction over native lands and resources. At the same time, the federal and provincial governments would retain those powers that would be exercised in the common interest of both natives and non-natives.

After decades of striving for self-government it would seem that the native leaders have almost reached their goal. The federal government has stated that they recognize in the aboriginal peoples, through their leadership, a clear desire for self-government. The federal government in its September 1991 constitutional proposals wrote,

> ... that aboriginal peoples be guaranteed a court-enforceable right to self-government. Over a period of up to ten years, aboriginal peoples and governments can negotiate self-government agreements. The right to self-government would be included in the Constitution now, to be enforced by the courts after this transition period.[4]

Some native leaders were angry because the proposal did not outrightly say that Canada recognizes the inherent right to native self-government. They also rejected the ten-year timetable as being too long. The Minister of Constitutional Affairs, the Rt. Hon. Joe Clark, replied,

> *What we are trying to do in these matters is to be pragmatic and find things that we can get accepted so we do not just talk about change, we achieve change ... But the most serious problem is the Canadian people. They are frightened of the concept of native self-government. To go too far too fast would only jeopardize the good will that exists. This is a field that is both controversial and difficult.*[5]

My experience in church leadership helps me to understand Mr. Clark's position. To clearly define and bring about all that native self-government entails is enormous and complicated. It is better to make the changes slowly, because we know people are often resistant to change. On the other hand, though, we should trust that the native leaders have done their homework and are ready to make changes.

Though I fully support native self-government, I do have two personal concerns. First, not all native groups are interested in self-government now or feel capable of administering their affairs today. Much of the agitation for sovereignty comes from reserves that already have a sound economic base and proven leadership.

Second, I'm concerned that non-natives assume that all native peoples trust in the traditional beliefs associated with Indians. Native Christians should speak out about their religious convictions to the media, helping them understand the importance of Christian faith to many aboriginals. But also, I would like to note that becoming a Christian does not in any way take away from our native culture. God gave each group their own culture, and he uses the people's culture to bring them to himself. As native Christians we should not be afraid to stand up for our rights in the kingdom of God.

Finally, I'm thankful to the Canadian government for many

things we may have taken for granted. Canada is a free country, and there is peace in our land. There are many countries in the world that would like to have the benefits we so freely enjoy. While the government has not always met our expectations, let's be grateful for the good they have done. If we work in cooperation with each other as natives and non-natives, I believe we can make Canada an even better country.

---

1. Carol Goar, "Why Ottawa's Plan Has Natives Angry," the *Toronto Star* (September 28, 1991).

2. James S. Frideres, *Native Peoples in Canada: Contemporary Conflicts* (Scarborough, Ont.: Prentice-Hall Canada Inc., 1988), p. 343.

3. *Ibid.,* pp. 344-358.

4. *Shaping Canada's Future Together,* Highlights, Minister of Supply and Services Canada, 1991, p. 5.

5. The *Toronto Star,* September 28, 1991.

THE CHARTER'S ROLE IN SHAPING CANADIAN VALUES

Peter Jervis

The introduction of the Charter of Rights and Freedoms into the Canadian Constitution in 1982 marked a profound change in Canadian political and cultural history. Although few Canadians realized it at the time, the Charter's introduction in 1982 was the forerunner to a fundamentally different constitutional framework in which the courts, rather than the politicians, would become the final arbiters of constitutional, cultural, and political values. Experience since 1982 has shown that the Charter has required the courts to intervene increasingly in what many would consider issues in which they should not be involved, and to make decisions that overturn the centuries-old political, cultural, and religious traditions upon which Canadian society was founded.

Recently the Ontario Court of Appeal held that provincial legislation requiring religious instruction in public schools is unconstitutional. Also, the Supreme Court of Canada has decided that the Lord's Day Act, mandating a common sabbath, was unconstitutional, because it impeded the freedom of religion of Canadians who do not observe the Christian sabbath.

However, that same constitutional right of religious freedom did not protect the rights of a fundamentalist minister in Alberta to educate his children in the home rather than sending them to a secular public school. Similarly, the concerns of anti-abortion activist Joe Borowski, who raised the issue of whether the developing life of the child *in utero* is worthy of constitutional protection, were not given constitutional protection.

It is apparent to many constitutional lawyers that our constitutional law is changing very rapidly. Through this process the courts are developing constitutional principles that will not only inform the basic values of our society but will indeed construct the very framework of our society.

These principles, now being developed by the courts on a subjective case-by-case basis, are crystallizing into immutable doctrines against which all future laws will be measured.

Christians must recognize that whereas it developed as a primarily "Christian" society in the eighteenth and nineteenth centuries, with much of its law, custom, and culture founded on Judeo-Christian values, Canada today is a multicultural society. Many ethnic minorities claim not only constitutional exemption from laws founded upon the Judeo-Christian tradition, but also insist that those laws must be reinterpreted or even abolished if Canada is to conform to a secular mosaic.

Thus, in a recent decision that prohibited the use of the Lord's Prayer in Ontario schools, the Ontario Court of Appeal determined that the developing principles of constitutional law "compel" the re-evaluation of this practice. The court stated bluntly: "It can no longer be assumed that Christian practices are acceptable to the whole community."

Those involved in this crucial constitutional process are acutely aware of the importance of participating in order to exert influence over the process. It is essential that those who seek to maintain for Canada a legal, constitutional, and cultural tradition founded upon Christian values participate actively in this process of constitutional litigation. Christians in the past may have assumed that their majoritarian views would predominate and free them from obligations to participate actively in the political or legal arena, but this is no longer the case.

The process of constitutional litigation is a dynamic and formative one. Judges must interpret our new Constitution and apply it to existing laws. This process requires judges to pour meaning into empty or vague constitutional phraseology, often without the assistance of previous judgments. If Christians desire the development of the Constitution in a manner consistent with their values and world view, they must shed their reluctance or condescension towards the legal process and become active participants.

They can do it either by initiating cases to assert or preserve their constitutional rights or by intervening in cases before the courts to ensure that their particular perspectives are heard. Many courts will welcome such participation when confronted with complex and difficult, value-laden decisions.

This is a particularly crucial period in the development of the Canadian Constitution. Vague intellectual concepts are crystallizing, through this process of judicial decision-making, into a set of principles upon which future laws and practices will be judged. If the processes of constitutional interpretation and formation are left to those who do not share religious, spiritual, or Christian values, then the basic framework of our society for years to come may be irrevocably altered.

This is a challenge to all concerned Canadians which demands a response.

This article is adapted from an article first appearing in *Christian Week*, May 30, 1989. Used with permission.

BIBLE STUDIES ON CHRISTIAN NATION-BUILDING

Darrel Reid and Brian Stiller

INTRODUCTION

It is important that we search the Scriptures to learn what God has to say about our nation and country. The following studies illustrate some of the biblical principles the Task Force on Canada's Future see as being important. They have been designed to serve either as a study series for Christian education classes or as subject material for sermons. They are not definitive, but rather serve as a guide to the subject.

In studying the Bible, it is important that we remind ourselves of the care required in examining what the Bible says and how that applies to today. As Christians we have the Bible to give us guidance as to how we are to think, pray, and speak as we live out our faith. And that includes how we respond to the crisis of Canada's future.

As Christians – we are sometimes called "People of the Book" – we believe that what the Bible says is critical for life. That is why we encourage the study of the Scriptures as a guide to assist us in making God-oriented choices about how we should think and pray about our country and its future.

However, a danger in looking into the Bible for answers to Canada's problems is to assume that what God says to Israel applies directly to Canada.

Israel was a nation particularly chosen to be the vehicle through which the Son of God would be revealed. God called Abraham to begin a nation that would eventually become Israel. In the Old Testament there are specific promises and commands given to Israel. In other words, Israel had a special place in God's plan for salvation. When we employ the Bible to help understand today's issues, we must read carefully what it really says. This is especially critical as we pray for our nation during this time of national crisis. We must keep in mind that Canada, though very much of concern to God, is not Israel.

It would be a mistake to take a promise and apply it in the same way to Canada today as it was intended for Israel. That does not mean the basic principles underlying the promise do not speak to us today. But it is important that Bible study principles be observed.

As you study the suggested texts, ask these questions:
1. Who wrote or was speaking?
2. To whom was it written?
3. What was the particular context? That is, what was going on at the time?
4. What would the readers or listeners understand those words to mean?
5. What are the basic principles underlying the message?
6. Am I forcing the Bible to say for today what was never intended in the first place?
7. In what ways can the basic message be applied to Canada today?

May God, through the Holy Spirit, guide you as you seriously examine God's Word as it speaks to us in these days.

I.   THE BLESSING PROMISED
Title: Is Canada God's Concern?
Theme:
   Nations, including Canada, can receive God's blessing.

This blessing, however, is conditional upon the response of his people.

Text: II Chronicles 7:14:

"If my people, who are called by my name, will humble themselves and pray and seek my face and turn from their wicked ways, then I will hear from heaven and will forgive their sin and will heal their land."

Background:

In this passage Solomon, son of King David, has just dedicated the Temple in Jerusalem, and God has manifested his presence. Then he speaks to Solomon. His words, spoken to Solomon and the nation of Israel, suggest principles that are of relevance to Canada today. In his message there is both a promise and a warning.

Outline for Text:

1. The Setting for blessing.

a. God calls his people to respond. God does not expect those who deny or ignore him to be obedient; obedience, rather, begins "in the house of the Lord." God expects those who are called by his name to have a sensitivity for the spiritual implications of current events. See, for example, 2 Kings 6:8-23.

b. God listens to the prayers of his people. "Does Canada matter to God?" is a question worth asking. When his people turn to him, he promises to listen. But does God concern himself with nations, boundaries, and even constitutions? In Acts 17:26-28 we see not only that God has established times and locations for the nations, but that these are part of his redemptive plan for humanity.

2. The conditions for blessing.

a. Self-initiated humility. It is one thing for someone else to humble us, but God calls upon Christians to humble themselves. Christ emphasizes the importance of such humility in such passages as Matthew 18:4 and Matthew

23:12: *"For whoever exalts himself will be humbled, and whoever humbles himself will be exalted."*

b. God's people must pray. Prayer is something that God's people are more likely to talk about than do! The assumption in this passage is that this prayer is more than merely a weekly shopping list for God. His people must *seek* him. This suggests a determined effort to go after God. Relevant passages are found in Psalm 27:8, Amos 5:14 and Luke 11:9: *"So I say to you, Ask and it will be given to you; seek and you will find; knock and the door will be opened to you."*

c. God's people must repent of and turn from sin. Only when the people of Israel recognized sinful attitudes and ways of life, confessed them and repented of them did God bless them. An example of national confession and repentance at a time of stress and testing is found in Isaiah 59:1-21: *"So justice is far from us, and righteousness does not reach us. We look for light, but all is darkness; for brightness, but we walk in deep shadows. Like the blind we grope along the wall ... For our offenses are many in your sight, and our sins testify against us. Our offenses are ever with us, and we acknowledge our iniquities ...."*

3. The promise of blessing.

God's blessing comes in two forms:

a. Forgiveness. The release of the burden of individual and collective guilt releases energy to pursue goodness. Note that it is not only a general forgiveness but a forgiveness rooted in relationship to others. Christ links forgiveness from God with our forgiveness for others; see Matthew 6:9-15 and Luke 6:37.

b. Healing. As it undoubtedly was for the nation of Israel, so it is for Canada. There are so many ways in which this land is sick. This sickness extends from individual sin and injustice through our corporate and political institutions to the land itself. God's word to the prophet Hosea (4:1-3) is that because of sin "*the land mourns ... the beasts of the field ... the birds of the sky ... the fish of the sea disappear.*" When sin rules in the land, even the environment is destroyed. There is need for healing of hearts and of the land.

Questions:

1. What are some of the reasons that this nation needs healing?

2. Many of the issues in Canada's constitutional debate have at their heart the perception of historic wrongs. Aboriginal peoples, minority language and ethnic groups, among others, have asked that these wrongs be addressed. Can the biblical pattern of repentance, prayer, forgiveness, and healing apply here? If so, how?

3. Can we expect politicians to solve Canada's problems when, at bottom, the country's hurt and sickness may be due to the unwillingness of people to call upon God?

Application:

Though we see about us various government policies with which we might disagree, the basic reason Canada struggles to survive is more spiritual than economic, cultural, or political. God's call comes first to his people. What is to be our response?

Prayer:

One suggestion is a prayer, either written out for the people of God to read together at the end of the service or study or else prayed by three persons, involving three aspects:

1. Prayer for willing and humble hearts.

2. Prayer for life-styles that include time for prayer.

3. Prayer for obedient hearts to turn from our sin(s).

II. THE GOODNESS EXPECTED

Title: What Does God Expect of Canada?

Theme:

God expects a nation to be characterized by justice, righteousness and compassion. His blessings will flow to all members of society in a land that loves and honours these principles.

Text: Psalm 72:

"Endow the King with your justice, O God, the royal son with righteousness.

2. *He will judge your people in righteousness, your afflicted ones with justice.*

3. *The mountains will bring prosperity to the people, the hills the fruit of righteousness.*

4. *He will defend the afflicted among the people and save the children of the needy; he will crush the oppressor.*

5. *He will endure as long as the sun, as long as the moon, through all generations.*

6. *He will be like rain falling on a mown field, like showers watering the earth.*

7. *In his days the righteous will flourish; prosperity will abound till the moon is no more.*

8. *He will rule from sea to sea and from the river to the ends of the earth.*

9. *The desert tribes will bow before him and his enemies will lick the dust.*

10. *The kings of Tarshish and of distant shores will bring tribute to him; the kings of Sheba and Seba will pre sent him gifts.*

11. *All kings will bow down to him and all nations will serve him.*

12. *For he will deliver the needy who cry out, the afflicted who have no one to help.*

13. *He will take pity on the weak and the needy and save the needy from death.*

14. *He will rescue them from oppression and violence, for precious is their blood in his sight.*

15. *Long may he live! May gold from Sheba be given him.*

> *May people ever pray for him and bless him all day long.*
>
> *16. Let grain abound throughout the land; on the tops of the hills may it sway. Let its fruit flourish like Lebanon; let it thrive like the grass of the field.*
>
> *17. May his name endure forever; may it continue as long as the sun. All nations will be blessed through him, and they will call him blessed.*
>
> *18. Praise be to the Lord God, the God of Israel, who alone does marvelous deeds.*
>
> *19. Praise be to his glorious name forever; may the whole earth be filled with his glory, Amen and Amen.*
>
> *20. This concludes the prayers of David son of Jesse."*

Background:

This is David's last psalm. In the final moments of his life he reflects upon nationhood and the qualities God expects of those who would seek his blessings.

Outline for text:

1. God seeks a nation built upon justice and righteousness.

These themes can be seen throughout the Old and New testaments. *"Endow the king with your justice, O God, the royal son with your righteousness. He will judge your people in righteousness, your afflicted ones with justice. The mountains will bring prosperity to the people, the hills the fruit of righteousness"* (vv. 1-3).

a. Justice. God calls his followers to seek equitable and right relations among all members of society. One of the prime characteristics of the kingdom of God is that it will be just, and God expects that love for justice to be reflected in its leaders. In Canada we are able to choose who those leaders are. In doing so, it is our responsibility to seek justice for all members of society. Zechariah 7:8-10 reads: *"This is what the Lord almighty says: Administer true justice; show mercy and compassion to one another.*

Do not oppress the widow or the fatherless, the alien or the poor. In your hearts do not think evil of each other." This justice does not just happen of itself. It requires action on the part of the faithful; see, for example, Psalm 82:3-4.

b. Righteousness. This term comes from a Hebrew word denoting something straight, whether referring to weights and measures or paths to be traveled. As Christians we are to consider our actions in light of God's standards for action as revealed in his Word. Isaiah 42:6-7 reads: "*I, the Lord, have called you in righteousness; I will take hold of your hand. I will keep you and will make you to be a covenant for the people ....*"

Lessons:

1. God expects justice and righteousness both from those who make the laws and enforce them and from those who are to follow them.

2. People are to know that their leaders will be fair in determining what is just within what they know is the standard.

3. These standards are to be clear and made public.

4. They are to reflect what the nation believes to be true.

2. *The godly nation will be characterized by compassion.*

"*He will defend the afflicted among the people and save the children of the needy; he will crush the oppressor .... For he will deliver the needy who cry out, the afflicted who have no one to help. He will take pity on the weak and the needy and save the needy from death ....*" (vv. 4, 13-14).

Although we Canadians have created huge, faceless bureaucracies to handle our welfare system, this does not relieve us of the responsibility for hearing God's call to compassion. Christian compassion is the practical application of Christian love which flows from God. In our "wel-

70

fare society" we, as Christians, must not lose sight of God's call to compassion for those who suffer, whether economically, physically, or spiritually. In Christ's parable of the Good Samaritan his point is driven home with a question, *"Which of these three do you think was a neighbour to the man who fell into the hands of thieves?"* (Luke 10:36).

Lessons:

1. Both those in leadership and those who have put them there are to be mindful of those in need, weakened, or unable to help themselves.

2. Nations are evaluated by God according to how they deal with the marginalized. He holds us, as Christian Canadians, responsible. This should be reflected in our attitudes toward government.

3. God's concern for a nation has an economic component.

"The mountains will bring prosperity to the people, the hills the fruit of righteousness ...

"Let grain abound throughout the land; on the tops of the hills may it sway. Let its fruit flourish like Lebanon; Let it thrive like the grass of the field" (vv. 3, 16).

Prosperity. In this psalm we see that God, who is sovereign over all things, is thus sovereign over the material prosperity of the godly nation. Note, however, that this prosperity is to be seen in the context of verse 12: *"For he will deliver the needy who cry out, the afflicted who have no one to help."*

God's material blessings to a nation are linked to his concern for justice and righteousness. The implication of this passage is that God's material blessing comes to nations actively concerned with the welfare of those least able to care for or defend themselves. Neither justice/righteousness nor economic well-being is reserved just for the few.

71

Lessons:

    1. God is concerned about economic relations in a country; his blessing is tied to his requirements to do justice.

    2. Material blessings are to be for all – not just a few.

Questions:

    1. Do God's standards for Israel, as reflected in David's prayer, have any application to Canada today?

    2. Does the call to care for the marginalized apply to Canadians today?

    3. How can one apply these scriptural principles today without being trapped by a particular ideology of economics or politics?

Application:

    Although each of us has differing views on politics and economics, God desires that national laws and policies be fair and just in their application and based on known standards.

    We who live in a democracy have a responsibility to see that these laws and policies reflect God's will for a godly nation.

Prayer:

    1. That we will treat others with fairness and justice.

    2. That we will support policies which are just.

    3. That as a nation we will seek righteousness and compassion as defined by God.

    4. That we will not spend our time and energy on what is just for ourselves, but we will look for justice for others.

III.   THE LEADERS AND FOLLOWERS REQUIRED

Title: Leading and Following

Theme:

    God has set into place, by his creation, governments to lead and serve. Christians honour God as they give honour to those God has set in authority over us. Those in authority, however, hold it in trust and must be reminded whose power they hold.

Text: Romans 13:1-8:

1. *Everyone must submit himself to the governing authorities, for there is no authority except that which God has established. The authorities that exist have been established by God.*

2. *Consequently, those who rebel against that authority is rebelling against what God has instituted, and so will bring judgment on themselves.*

3. *For rulers hold no terror for those who do right, but for those who do wrong. Do you want to be free from fear of the one in authority? Then do what is right and he will commend you.*

4. *For he is God's servant to do you good. But if you do wrong, be afraid, for he does not bear the sword for nothing. He is God's servant, an agent of wrath to bring punishment on the wrongdoer.*

5. *Therefore, it is necessary to submit to the authorities, not only because of possible punishment but also because of conscience.*

6. *This is also why you pay taxes, for the authorities are God's servants, who give their full time to governing.*

7. *Give everyone what you owe him: If you owe taxes, pay taxes; if revenue, then revenue; if respect, then respect; if honour, then honour.*

8. *Let no debt remain outstanding, except the continuing debt to love one another, for he who loves his fellow man has fulfilled the law.*

Background:

Most people read verses 1-6 without reading both the chapter that precedes them and the verses that follow. In Chapter 12 Paul reminds the Romans not to be conformed to the world, to love others, to bless their persecutors, to

73

avoid repaying evil for evil, and to overcome evil with good. In Romans 13 Paul sets his discussion of authority within the context of verse 8: *"Let no debt remain outstanding, except the continuing debt to love one another, for he who loves his fellow man has fulfilled the law."*

Outline for Text:

1. Governments are God's creation.

"For rulers hold no terror for those who do right, but for those who do wrong. Do you want to be free from fear of the one in authority? Then do what is right and he will commend you. For he is God's servant to do you good" (vv. 3-4a).

a. Political authority is authority from God. The Scriptures teach that all things *"in heaven, and on earth, visible and invisible, whether thrones or powers or rulers or authorities; all things were created by him and for him"* (Colossians 1:16).

b. This authority is bound by God's task for governments: to do good. In writing these words, Paul understood that the Roman government could not always be counted upon to do good. Here Paul is outlining the role and responsibility for governments.

c. A government is not a god. It is, rather, to be a servant. Its role is circumscribed by its twin responsibilities, found in I Peter 2:14, of punishing the evildoer and commending good.

Lessons:

1. Christians are called to affirm the dignity of the office of government as God's creation.

2. When governments act within their mandate of suppressing evil and doing good, they are acting as servants of God. This applies even at times when we do not agree with particular policies.

3. Governments are bound, however, by the mandate God

has given them. They are responsible to him for how it is carried out.

2. We, as followers of Christ, are to be responsible citizens.

"Give everyone what you owe him: If you owe taxes, pay taxes; if revenue, then revenue; if respect, then respect; if honor, then honor. Let no debt remain outstanding except the continuing debt to love one another, for he who loves his fellow man has fulfilled the law" (vv. 7-8).

a. We are to honour those in authority over us. This concept seems somewhat remote, given the poisoned political environment we see about us. In our conversations with others, however, it is important to remember Paul's advice to Titus: *"Remind the people to be subject to rulers and authorities, to be obedient, to be ready to do whatever is good, to slander no one, to be peaceable and considerate, and to show true humility toward all men"* (Titus 3:1,2).

b. We are to remind governments of their responsibilities before God. In doing this we, as followers of Christ, discharge to governments the "debt of love" we are to have for one another (Romans 13:8). For we respectfully declare to them the nature of ultimate spiritual reality: *"Be still and know that I am God; I will be exalted among the nations, I will be exalted in the earth"* (Psalm 46:10).

Lessons:

1. Christians are to be obedient to God's injunction to be responsible citizens.

2. We do this by bearing faithful witness to governments of their responsibility before God and their place within his creation.

Questions:

1. What sorts of attitudes towards leadership do we see around us? To what extent have they played a role in our country's current situation?

2. How would you describe your view of government?

3. How would your close associates describe your view of government, from what they have heard you say?

Application:

The nasty spirit of our culture towards those who lead in government has spilled over into the church. Christians, who should be reflecting God's perspectives as found in the Bible and confirmed by the Holy Spirit, need to examine their own attitudes and reflect upon what they say, especially during moments of disagreement.

Prayer:

1. For those in authority, beginning with the prime minister.

2. Pray that they would have integrity and honesty in the decisions they make.

3. Pray that God would enable us to go to the Scriptures to let them illumine the attitudes of our hearts.

4. Pray that our nation would be blessed by God as those who bear the name of Christ seek to reflect his love and light to those around us and to those who are in authority over us.

PARTICIPATING IN CONSTITUTIONAL DEBATE

Don Page

Canada needs people with vision and insight, who are willing to help improve understanding of the various problems and offer constructive solutions. We are fortunate in Canada to be living under governments that seek and receive our input into the affairs of state and the making of public policy. In fact, governments spend millions of tax dollars each year trying to find out what we want them to do.

Many of us have been slow to realize our responsibilities and opportunities as citizens to influence government policy through the tools of democracy. The ballot box is not the only, nor the most effective, way to influence governments, though it may provide the ultimate sanction.

In a pluralistic society we cannot force our views on others, but through persuasion we can influence the future by having a seat or voice at the decision-making table. Otherwise others will make the decisions that affect our daily lives without regard to Christian values. Like Jonah, we will fail to live as Christ's ambassadors to a needy world.

The individuals who are charged with the responsibility of governing need wise counsel. Christians who are called into public life need our constant support, encouragement and prayers.

SOME SUGGESTIONS FOR EFFECTIVE INFLUENCE

1. Meet with your local Member of Parliament. Most citizens influence government most effectively through their elected representatives. All elected officials maintain offices in their constituencies. You have a right and responsibility to make your views known to them. Far from not wanting to hear from you, most elected officials complain that they do not hear *enough* from their constituents after they are elected. Especially important are those officials who sit on committees handling specific issues or bills and the cabinet ministers responsible for those issues.

2. Seek opportunities to participate in constitutional hearings or local conferences. Take initiatives in sponsoring a forum for discussion of national issues if no occasion arises otherwise.

3. In any encounter with government officials or people representing disparate views, be polite and pleasant. If confronted with a hostile reaction, don't get hurt or become combative. Remember that the nastiness or anger is usually not personal; it is directed at what the other person thinks you represent. Often this is more a matter of faulty understanding of what Christians represent or long-standing prejudices against them. Remember what Scripture says: "A soft answer turns away wrath." When you return their anger with sweetness you open the door to a hearing that a shouting match will never achieve. Let us never forget that this is the Lord's battle, not ours.

4. Always present your point of view on the basis of how it will benefit others, including the person to whom you are speaking. What may seem obviously right to Christians is seldom that obvious to non-Christians.

5. Do your homework. Know the issue and be prepared to present the probable consequences that will flow from not following your recommended course of action.

6. Understanding the issues involves more than collecting the relevant facts. Try to discuss controversial points such as native self-government and "distinct society" with people who are

directly affected; e.g., native people or francophones.

7. Do not assume that the media are automatically the enemy (nobody thinks the media treat them fairly). Reporters are human beings just as we are, with their own ways of looking at things. The reporter often relies on stereotypes because of the pressure to produce an instant story. If you have something new to say, be sure that that is made clear.

8. Do not be negative. No one likes a nagger or complainer. Start with something complimentary about what the government is doing or appreciation for its interest in trying to do what is right on this issue. From this foundation you are in a better position to gain a fair and open hearing for your particular concern.

9. Do not ignore the opposition by assuming that they will not want to hear your point of view. You never know where the weak point is in their armour or when you might strike a sympathetic chord. Never despair.

10. Do not be ashamed to stand for what you believe in. It is common to feel nervous or frightened before you make a telephone call or meet your MP. Such emotions will not discredit you; rather, they are seen as contributing to your sincerity and determination in making your views known.

11. Do not be defeated by your mistakes. We all make them when we try to do something worthwhile. This is the part of the learning experience that helps us improve.

12. Do not be apologetic about expressing your opinions. This is, after all, a democratic society in which the government goes to great lengths to find out what its citizens think about a host of diverse issues. Since you are going forth as Christ's ambassador, go prayerfully in his Spirit of boldness.

WRITING LETTERS TO GOVERNMENT

1. Write an individual letter. Form letters, coupons, or petitions are considered meaningless as expressions of concern by individual voters.

2. Use business letterhead, particularly if you are a president or senior officer of a company or organization. This gives your views credibility.

3. Your letter should do three things:
   a) outline the problem or the issue;
   b) state what you want done about the problem or issue, and;
   c) explain why the government should direct its attention to your concern at this particular time.

4. Be clear. State your views concisely. Avoid long, complicated arguments.

5. Be brief. Short, concise, one- or two-page letters are more likely to be read.

6. Capture the attention of busy politicians by quoting one of their statements on the issue. Point out the possible political consequences of their intended actions.

7. Ask for information about your MP's own views and his or her party's official position. Request a reply. If your MP's reply does not answer all of your questions, write a brief note back requesting replies to those items left unanswered. This will make him or her rethink the position.

8. If you write to the prime minister or a cabinet minister, send a copy to your own MP and a Christian MP. They can refer to it in caucus if no action is forthcoming.

9. Letters sent to MPs require no postage. In place of a stamp just write O.H.M.S. The letter should be addressed to your Member of Parliament, House of Commons, Ottawa, Ontario, K1A 0A6.

10. Encourage others to write letters.

11. Send the letter with a prayer that God would move the heart of the recipient, as in Proverbs 21:1.

12. Above all, be Christlike in attitude and word. Remember that the apostle Paul calls government leaders "ministers of God."

FOR FURTHER READING

Brian Stiller

There are a few books available that will be helpful as you examine how the Bible speaks to Christians living in a modern political nation. The challenge facing Canada is not unique, nor is it new. Christians in other countries have gone through the heart-wrenching task of participating in the reconstruction of their country. But in Canada we are so overwhelmed by American news that too often we are at a loss as to how we should relate to our own history and traditions.

Listed below are a few books, with notes on how they might be of help. Following that is a general listing of books under the three categories of Canadian church history, social and political analysis, and biblical/theological analysis.

The two books that give evangelicals the best insight into our past are *The Evangelical Century* (Michael Gauvreau, McGill-Queens University Press, 1991), and *The Canadian Protestant Experience* (George A. Rawlyk, ed., Welch Publishing Company Inc., 1990). Both show the importance of the evangelical community in thought and deed, especially in the nineteenth century. For those who think Canada has no strong evangelical heritage, these books, written by Canadian church historians, will show the contrary.

On the social side, Reg Bibby, professor of sociology at the

University of Lethbridge, has produced a definitive work on the Canadian church, *Fragmented Gods* (Stoddart, 1988). He traces the rise and mostly the fall of church and Christian influence in Canada. His book *Mosaic Madness* (Stoddart, 1990) is a look at the highly fragmented country Canada has become. Bibby does not have answers for what we should do about our cultural bits and pieces, but he does offer a serious analysis.

Thine is the Kingdom (Eerdmans, 1984) by Paul Marshall, professor of political theory at the Institute for Christian Studies, provides the most complete and helpful overview of a Christian view of politics. *The Naked Public Square* (Richard John Neuhaus, Eerdmans, 1984) outlines from an American point of view how public life has been stripped of its Christian garments. *Kingdoms in Conflict* (Charles Colson, Zondervan, 1987) is one of the most popular of Colson's writings. The title describes his thesis that the kingdom of Caesar and that of Christ are in conflict. Bob Goudzwaard in *Idols of our Time* (IVP, 1981) describes how subtly the ideologies of our culture become the idols of Christians.

Politics and the Biblical Drama by Richard Mouw (Baker, 1976) looks into the Old Testament and describes the relationship between humanity's fall and the surrounding political dynamics. Lesslie Newbigin's *The Gospel in a Pluralistic Society* (Eerdmans, 1989) describes the development of pluralism and offers a challenge to the church on its call to reach society. John Stott in his *Decisive Issues Facing Christians Today* (Revell, 1984) examines a number of issues, including political involvement, pluralism, the environment, human rights, feminism, and the like.

OTHER SELECTED BOOKS:
1. Canadian Church History
Ramsay Cook, *The Regenerators* (University of Toronto Press, 1985).

S. D. Clark, *Church and Sect in Canada* (University of Toronto Press, 1948).

S. Crysdale and L. Wheatcroft, eds., *Religion in Canadian Society* (Macmillan of Canada, 1976).

Brian J. Fraser, *The Social Uplifters* (Wilfrid Laurier University Press, 1988).

John Webster Grant, *The Church in the Canadian Era* (Welch Publishing Company, Inc., 1988).

John Webster Grant, *A Profusion of Spires* (University of Toronto Press, 1988).

John Webster Grant, ed., *The Churches and the Canadian Experience* (The Ryerson Press, 1963).

John Webster Grant, *Moon of Wintertime* (University of Toronto Press, 1984).

Marguerite Van Die, *An Evangelical Mind* (McGill-Queens University Press, 1989).

H.H. Walsh, *The Christian Church in Canada* (The Ryerson Press, 1956).

William Westfall, *Two Worlds* (McGill-Queens University Press, 1989).

2. Social and Political analysis

Harry Antonides, ed., *Servant or Tyrant?* (Christian Labour Association of Canada, 1989).

John Eidsmore, *God and Caesar* (Crossway Books, 1984).

Seymour Lipset, *Continental Divide* (Routledge, 1990).

Andrew H. Malcolm, *The Canadians* (Fitzhenry and Whiteside, 1985).

Glenn Tinder, *The Political Meaning of Christianity* (Harper Collins, 1989).

Robert Wuthnow, *The Struggle for America's Soul: Evangelicals, Liberals and Secularism* (Eerdmans).

3. Biblical/theological analysis

Robert Bellah, ed., *Post Modern Theology: Christian Faith in a Pluralist World* (Harper and Row, 1989).

Harry Blamires, *The Christian Mind* (Servant, 1963).

Harry Blamires, *The Secularist Heresy* (Servant, 1956).

Donald Bloesch, *The Future of Evangelical Christianity* (Doubleday, 1983).

John Bright, *The Kingdom of God* (Abingdon, 1981).

James Hitchcock, *What is Secular Humanism?* (Servant, 1982).

Donald B. Kraybill, *The Upside-Down Kingdom* (Herald Press, 1990).

Richard Lovelace, *Dynamics of Spiritual Life* (IVP, 1979).

David O. Moberg, *The Great Reversal* (Holman, 1977).

Lesslie Newbigin, *Foolishness to the Greeks* (Eerdmans, 1986).

Arthur Simon, *Christian Faith and Public Policy* (Eerdmans, 1987).

H. Richard Niebuhr, *Christ and Culture* (Harper Torchbooks, 1951).

Christopher Wright, *An Eye for An Eye* (IVP, 1983).

Appendix A

Submission
by the Evangelical Fellowship of Canada
to the Special Joint Committee
on a Renewed Canada

INTRODUCTION

The Evangelical Fellowship of Canada (EFC) is the national association of Canadian evangelicals, serving some 28 denominations in fields of national interest, including social and political concerns. It is estimated that there are two and a half million evangelicals in Canada. United in the belief that the Christian gospel has implications for how we can live together as Canadians, we are deeply concerned about the present crisis in Canada.

Christianity was fundamental in shaping the culture and institutions of Canada. Together with other religious faiths, it continues to influence the way Canadians understand themselves as a nation.

The values which undergird Canada's political institutions were first instilled by Christian beliefs. They are recognized to be true by people of Canada's many other faiths. These values must be reaffirmed and revitalized if Canadians are to shape their future together. The constitutional proposals formulated by the Government of Canada will flounder if they are not in tune with our most basic beliefs about who we are as Canadians.

CANADA'S RELIGIOUS TRADITION

Canada's identity – the distinctive features that set it apart in the world – has been deeply affected by Christian values. One aspect of this is that our founding constitutional documents reveal an acceptance of the diversity of peoples and cultures as a fundamental fact of political life. They represent the search for ways in which those peoples can live together harmoniously. Those who established the Canadian political union wanted, as Psalm 72 says, a "dominion" of peace and justice from sea to sea.

The idea of Canada having an identity – a sense of calling and an ordered place in the scheme of things – made some sense. As far as Ontario and the Maritimes were concerned, they thought that they were Christian, that they lay in a British tradition and that they were not American.

This has produced many Canadian myths, some of them true: "Peace, order and good government" over against the American "Life, liberty and the pursuit of happiness." Our lone Mountie keeping order over against the U.S. "Wild West." Our mild manners, our clean cities, our lower murder and crime rates – these have always been a source of Canadian pride. But none of this was, or needed to be, sustained by a created sense of identity. The identity was shaped by, amongst other things, a sense of Canada's vocation in a divinely ordered universe.

But Canada has not been simply a submissive and hierarchical society. It has also stressed individual freedom, responsibility and initiative. Indeed, what may be distinctively Canadian, or English-Canadian, is this balance of communal order and individual responsibility.

As recent research is showing, much of this stress on the individual came to the fore in Canada through the influence of evangelical Christianity. Evangelicalism has shaped much of Canada outside of Quebec. It remade the Maritimes and Ontario in the nineteenth century, and exerted tremendous influence on the development of the West in the twentieth century. It is a major and growing force among aboriginal peoples and new Canadians.

As it sought reform throughout society evangelicalism continually tried to tie communal order and personal responsibility together. Indeed, it can be said that the evangelical balance mirrors the Canadian balance.

Given that Canada's history and identity are tied to its religious history, any defense of Canada must necessarily contain some appreciation of that inheritance. If it is disregarded then a sense of Canada will be lost, to the detriment of all its people, whatever their religion. Robertson Davies has suggested that one possible root of the word *religion* is *religare* – to connect. Our present fragmentation as a country is tied to our neglect of that connectedness.

RELIGION IN CANADA'S FUTURE

We live in a pluralistic society. Different people with different beliefs and different ways of life now live together within our national boundaries. A good type of pluralism is one that enables us to live together in peace and mutual respect, while at the same time acknowledging that our differences are very real and important. One problem with much of the current stress on pluralism is that it tries to achieve a kind of peace either by denying that differences exist or by denying their importance. The result is that committed believers – of many religions – are told that they must leave their beliefs at the door if they want to enter public debate. Religion is excluded in the name of tolerance and openness to all.

This secularism then becomes a false form of pluralism. By trying to exclude religious considerations from public influence, it destroys the very diversity it claims to want to protect. It claims not to discriminate but ends up discriminating against any religion that shapes the public life of its members. At the same time it asserts values based only on mutual self-interest, which are not enough to hold a country together.

Constitutions are meant to reflect the fundamental political values of the citizens that are governed by them. When these fundamental values are ignored, rejected or altered without popular input and approval, strife will follow. Thus prospective changes must be evaluated by the degree to which they contribute to the strengthening of these values in the hearts and minds of the citizens.

As our contemporary political leaders have acknowledged, the values that have often made Canada the envy of others are rooted in our Judeo-Christian heritage. In 1981, Prime Minister Trudeau reminded Canadians that "the golden thread of faith is woven throughout the history of Canada ... It was in acknowledgment of that debt that the Parliament of Canada later gave its approval ... to the statement that Canada is founded upon principles that recognize the supremacy of God and the rule of law." To which the Rt. Hon. Joe Clark added, "I ask that we never forget the faith and the vision of the people who originally brought this country together."

Because of the relationship between religion, identity and our current political problems, we urge that the religious forces that shape our country be duly recognized in our constitutional discussions. They are not anachronisms that hinder our travel into a plural new world, but are part of the very fibre of who we are as a people and a country. As we seek to revise our Constitution together, we should do so in a way that enhances the place in Canadian society of religion and values which are held deeply.

AN EVANGELICAL CONTRIBUTION

As a means of helping to shape our nation, the Evangelical Fellowship of Canada wants to offer and suggest:

a) a national perspective based on a regionally and ethnically diverse membership, that is willing to work with Canadians from other faiths;

b) a means for national reconstruction through confession, forgiveness, restitution and lasting reconciliation based on the experience we have in trying to unite diverse groups and interests into a unified whole;

c) a more cooperative, less adversarial spirit in our political culture; and

d) a national vision of Canada that is based on common values for the common good.

While particular members of the Evangelical Fellowship of Canada can comment on the details of the proposed constitutional restructuring, we believe that the EFC's best contribution is to the values that are to be enshrined in the constitutional proposals. We believe that many of these values are rooted in God's revelation to all people and that, when tested, will be found to be applicable to all Canadians, regardless of their faith.

The values which should be reflected in our constitution would include the following:

1) Respect for proper authority and responsible leadership;

2) Responsible citizenship that recognizes diversity within our unity, while accomplishing common goals;

3) Integrity as a national goal;

4) Caring internationalism that is not overridden by economic nationalism;

5) Responsible stewardship of our environment for the integrity of God's creation and for future generations;

6) Compassion and justice as the motives for helping those who have been lost and hurt within society;

7) Importance of the family as the basis for a happy and productive community;

8) Freedom to seek what is good in life, in balance with personal and collective responsibilities;

9) Justice that is redemptive as well as punitive, but does not penalize the victims more than the perpetrators of crime; and

10) "Shalom" – a peace that promotes an all-encompassing relational harmony in society, rather than a "justice" which seeks merely to settle old scores, particularly when dealing with aboriginal and distinct societies.

THE CONSTITUTIONAL PROPOSALS

The values listed above would affect all of the amendments to the Constitution Act, 1867, as proposed by the Government of Canada. Our recommendations pertain particularly to the proposals which deal with the "Canada Clause," with Quebec and with aboriginal peoples.

I. On the Canada Clause (Proposal 7):

a) We applaud the recognition in the proposed clause of the importance of community, especially as it is articulated in the final phrase. We agree that "the balance that is especially Canadian between personal and collective freedom on the one hand and, on the other hand, the personal and collective responsibility that we all share with each other" ought to be reflected in the Canada clause. Furthermore, we agree that Canada cannot be understood or governed on the notion that Canadians are no more than a collection of discrete individuals.

b) We also affirm the Government's intention to entrench the clause within the body of the Constitution Act, 1867, rather than relegating it to preambular status, where it would serve only a symbolic, and not an interpretive, function.

c) We propose that a phrase be included in the Canada Clause which recognizes both the primary responsibility of parents for their children's nurture and education and the nation's responsibility for the protection and welfare of children and their families.

d) We make the following observations regarding the proposed wording of the Canada Clause:

i) *re* "a commitment to fairness, openness and full participation in Canada's citizenship by all people without regard to race, colour, creed, physical or mental disability, or cultural background": We recommend that the sentence end after "all people," since any attempt to have an all-inclusive list following "with regard to" will fail, and such an attempt creates more problems and politicking than it solves;

ii) *re* "recognition that the aboriginal peoples were historically self-governing": Such recognition is weak, and adds up to nothing for the present situation of aboriginal peoples;

iii) *re* "the contribution to the building of a strong Canada of peoples from many cultures and lands": We recommend that the phrase read, "from many cultures, lands and religions"; religion should be viewed as a distinct category, not to be subsumed under culture. People of different lands and cultures can share the same religious beliefs, and vice versa.

iv) *re* "our responsibility to preserve and protect the environment for future generations": We wish to point out that environmental stewardship is also important for the creation's own sake, not just in the interest of future generations;

v) *re* "respect for the rights of its citizens and constituent communities as set forth in the Canadian Charter of Rights and Freedoms": The Charter is not an exhaustive summary of rights. Some rights, such as those of aboriginal peoples or denominational schools, are not in the Charter, but are found in other sections of the Constitution. There are also rights under international treaties. Therefore, we suggest that the words "as set forth in the Canadian Charter of Rights and Freedoms" be deleted;

vi) *re* "the free flow of people, goods, services and capital throughout the Canadian economic union and the principle of equality of opportunity throughout Canada": We are concerned that the importance of other principles, such as economic equity, be recognized;

vii) *re* "a commitment to the well-being of all Canadians":

We would add "and people all over the world," in recognition of our international responsibilities; and

viii) *re* "a commitment to a democratic parliamentary system of government": We recommend a commitment also to developing more cooperative models of government, as a deliberate attempt to move away from the adversarial nature of much of current politics.

II. On the clauses dealing with aboriginal peoples (Proposals 3 to 6):
   a) We affirm that:
      i) native peoples have a distinct culture within Canada;
      ii) native peoples ought to be allowed to manage their own affairs within Confederation; and
      iii) native evangelicals generally support native leaders in promoting aboriginal self-government.

   b) We believe that all dealings with Canada's aboriginal peoples should reflect the values which we have set out, e.g., the importance of recognizing diversity within unity; the importance of recognizing communities, not just individuals; and the importance of establishing harmonious relationships between communities. These values should shape not only the desired result of self-government but also the process of achieving it. The historic pattern of government domination and discrimination can no longer continue.

III. On the "distinct society" clause (Proposal 2):
   a) Regarding the proposed amendment to the Canadian Charter of Rights and Freedoms, which would stipulate that the "Charter shall be interpreted in a manner consistent with ... the preservation and promotion of Quebec as a distinct society within Canada," we note that Quebec is not a homogeneous society, but itself includes a mix of faith and value cultures and communities. This should be reflected in the Charter amendment.

   b) Our suggested value of achieving "shalom" or "all-encompassing relational harmony" should be applied in all dealings with Quebec. We must get beyond the mechanical, score-card approach to justice, recognizing that many times strict equality does not equate with justice. As the Ontario Crown Employees Grievance Settlement Board wrote in a recent ruling, "Sometimes, in order to treat people equally, it is necessary to treat them differently." A shalom-like approach to justice is not foreign to the Canadian political tradition: the Confederation agreements with Manitoba (1890) and Newfoundland (1949) recognized both new provinces' unique educational arrangements.

CONCLUSION

For far too long we as a nation have been focusing on what divides us, or on what is novel, rather than on what creates and unites a healthy nation and society. Let us not forget that a nation and its mission is like a garden; it has to be constantly cultivated and watered if it is to flourish. The spiritual attitude which must underlie each person's and each community's search for a better way of living cannot be ignored and must be allowed to flourish in our land.

As representatives of a nation-wide evangelical community we submit our contribution to the current debate. We do not profess to have a great portion of the answers to our current national malaise, but our roots are deeply imbedded in the life of our nation. We sincerely want to do our part in helping to build a national community of communities based on essential values that will unite all Canadians from sea to sea. To this end we would be pleased to be called upon to assist in the process of "shaping our future together."

October 28, 1991

Appendix B

Canadian Charter of Rights and Freedoms

GUARANTEE OF RIGHTS AND FREEDOMS
1. The Canadian Charter of Rights and Freedoms guarantees the rights and freedoms set out in it subject only to such reasonable limits prescribed by laws as can be demonstrably justified in a free and democratic society.

FUNDAMENTAL FREEDOMS
2. Everyone has the following fundamental freedoms:
    (a) freedom of conscience and religion;
    (b) freedom of thought, belief, opinion and expression, including freedom of the press and other media of communication;
    (c) freedom of peaceful assembly; and
    (d) freedom of association.

DEMOCRATIC RIGHTS
3. Every citizen of Canada has the right to vote in an election of members of the House of Commons or of a legislative assembly and to be qualified for membership therein.

4. (1) No House of Commons and no legislative assembly shall continue for longer than five years from the date fixed for the return of the writs at a general election of its members.
    (2) In time of real or apprehended war, invasion or insurrection, a

House of Commons may be continued by Parliament and a legislative assembly may be continued by the legislature beyond five years if such continuation is not opposed by the votes of more than one-third of the members of the House of Commons or the legislative assembly, as the case may be.

5. There shall be a sitting of Parliament and of each legislature at least once every twelve months.

MOBILITY RIGHTS
6. (1) Every citizen of Canada has the right to enter, remain in and leave Canada.

(2) Every citizen of Canada and every person who has the status of a permanent resident of Canada has the right

    (a) to move to and take up residence in any province; and

    (b) to pursue the gaining of a livelihood in any province.

(3) The rights specified in subsection (2) are subject to

    (a) any laws or practices of general application in force in a province other than those that discriminate among persons primarily on the basis of province of present or previous residence; and

    (b) any laws providing for reasonable residency requirements as a qualification for the receipt of publicly provided social services.

(4) Subsections (2) and (3) do not preclude any law, program or activity that has as its object the amelioration in a province of conditions of individuals in that province who are socially or economically disadvantaged if the rate of employment in that province is below the rate of employment in Canada.

LEGAL RIGHTS
7. Everyone has the right to life, liberty and security of the person and the right not to be deprived thereof except in accordance with the principles of fundamental justice.

8. Everyone has the right to be secure against unreasonable search or seizure.

9. Everyone has the right not to be arbitrarily detained or imprisoned.

10. Everyone has the right on arrest or detention
    (a) to be informed promptly of the reasons therefor;
    (b) to retain and instruct counsel without delay and to be informed of that right; and
    (c) to have the validity of the detention determined by way of *habeas corpus* and to be released if the detention is not lawful.

11. Any person charged with an offence has the right
    (a) to be informed without unreasonable delay of the specific offence;
    (b) to be tried within a reasonable time;
    (c) not to be compelled to be a witness in proceedings against that person in respect of the offence;
    (d) to be presumed innocent until proven guilty according to law in a fair and public hearing by an independent and impartial tribunal;
    (e) not to be denied reasonable bail without just cause;
    (f) except in the case of an offence under military law tried by a military tribunal, to the benefit of trial by jury where the maximum punishment for the offence is imprisonment for five years or a more severe punishment;
    (g) not to be found guilty on account of any act or omission unless, at the time of the act or omission, it constituted an offence under Canadian or international law or was criminal according to the general principles of law recognized by the community of nations;
    (h) if finally acquitted of the offence, not to be tried for it again and, if finally found guilty and punished for the offence, not to be tried or punished for it again; and
    (i) if found guilty of the offence and if the punishment for the offence has been varied between the time of commission and the time of sentencing, to the benefit of the lesser punishment.

12. Everyone has the right not to be subjected to any cruel and unusual treatment or punishment.

13. A witness who testifies in any proceedings has the right not to have any incriminating evidence so given used to incriminate that witness in any other proceedings, except in a prosecution for perjury or for the giving of contradictory evidence.

14. A party or witness in any proceedings who does not understand or speak the language in which the proceedings are conducted or who is deaf has the right to the assistance of an interpreter.

EQUALITY RIGHTS

15.(1) Every individual is equal before and under the law and has the right to the equal protection and equal benefit of the law without discrimination and, in particular, without discrimination based on race, national or ethnic origin, colour, religion, sex, age or mental or physical disability.

(2) Subsection (1) does not preclude any law, program or activity that has as its object the amelioration of conditions of disadvantaged individuals or groups including those that are disadvantaged because of race, national or ethnic origins, colour, religion, sex, age or mental or physical disability.

OFFICIAL LANGUAGES OF CANADA

16.(1) English and French are the official languages of Canada and have equality of status and equal rights and privileges as to their use in all institutions of the Parliament and government of Canada.

(2) English and French are the official languages of New Brunswick and have equality of status and equal rights and privileges as to their use in all institutions of the legislature and government of New Brunswick.

(3) Nothing in this Charter limits the authority of Parliament or a legislature to advance the equality of status or use of English and French.

17.(1) Everyone has the right to use English and French in any debates and other proceedings of Parliament.

(2) Everyone has the right to use English and French in any debates and other proceedings of the legislature of New Brunswick.

18.(1) The statutes, records and journals of Parliament shall be printed and published in English and French and both language versions are equally authoritative.

(2) The statutes, records and journals of the legislature of New Brunswick shall be printed and published in English and French and both language versions are equally authoritative.

19.(1) Either English or French may be used by any person in, or in any pleading in or process issuing from, any court established by Parliament.

(2) Either English or French may be used by any person in, or in any pleading in or process issuing from, any court of New Brunswick.

20.(1) Any member of the public of Canada has the right to communicate with, and to receive available services from, any head or central office of an institution of the Parliament or government of Canada in English or French, and has the same right with respect to any other office of any such institution where

(a) there is a significant demand for communications with and services from that office in such language; or
(b) due to the nature of the office, it is reasonable that communications with and services from that office be available in both English and French.

(2) Any member of the public of New Brunswick has the right to communicate with, and to receive available services from, any office of an institution of the legislature or government of New Brunswick in English or French.

21. Nothing in sections 16 to 20 abrogates or derogates from any right, privilege or obligation with respect to the English and French languages, or either of them, that exists or is continued by virtue of any other provision of the Constitution of Canada.

22. Nothing in sections 16 to 20 abrogates or derogates from any legal or customary right or privilege acquired or enjoyed either before or after the coming into force of this Charter with respect to any language that is not English or French.

MINORITY LANGUAGE EDUCATIONAL RIGHTS

23.(1) Citizens of Canada
    (a) whose first language learned and still understood is that of the English or French linguistic minority population of the province in which they reside, or
    (b) who have received their primary school instruction in Canada in English or French and reside in a province where the language in which they received that instruction is the language of the English or French linguistic minority population of the province,
have the right to have their children receive primary and secondary school instruction in that language in that province.

(2) Citizens of Canada of whom any child has received or is receiving primary or secondary school instruction in English or French in Canada have the right to have all their children receive primary and secondary school instruction in the same language.

(3) The right of citizens of Canada under subsections (1) and (2) to have their children receive primary and secondary school instruction in the language of the English or French linguistic minority population of a province
    (a) applies wherever in the province the number of children of citizens who have such a right is sufficient to warrant the provision to them out of public funds of minority language instruction; and
    (b) includes, where the number of those children so warrants, the right to have them receive that instruction in minority language education facilities provided out of public funds.

ENFORCEMENT

24.(1) Anyone whose rights or freedoms, as guaranteed by this Charter, have been infringed or denied may apply to a court of competent jurisdiction to obtain such remedy as the court considers appropriate and just in the circumstances.

(2) Where, in proceedings under subsection (1), a court concludes that evidence was obtained in a manner that infringed or denied any rights or freedoms guaranteed by this Charter, the evidence shall be excluded if it is established that, having regard to all the circumstances, the admission of it in the proceedings would bring the administration of justice into disrepute.

GENERAL

25. The guarantee in this Charter of certain rights and freedoms shall not be construed so as to abrogate or derogate from any aboriginal, treaty or other rights or freedoms that pertain to the aboriginal peoples of Canada including

(a) any rights or freedoms that have been recognized by the Royal Proclamation of October 7, 1763; and

(b) any rights or freedoms that may be acquired by the aboriginal peoples of Canada by way of land claims settlement.

26. The guarantee in this Charter of certain rights and freedoms shall not be construed as denying the existence of any other rights or freedoms that exist in Canada.

27. This Charter shall be interpreted in a manner consistent with the preservation and enhancement of the multicultural heritage of Canadians.

28. Notwithstanding anything in this Charter, the rights and freedoms referred to in it are guaranteed equally to male and female persons.

29. Nothing in this Charter abrogates or derogates from any rights or privileges guaranteed by or under the Constitution of Canada in respect of denominational, separate or dissentient schools.

30. A reference in this Charter to a province or to the legislative assembly or legislature of a province shall be deemed to include a ref-

erence to the Yukon Territory and the Northwest Territories, or to the appropriate legislative authority thereof, as the case may be.

31. Nothing in this Charter extends the legislative powers of any body or authority.

APPLICATION OF CHARTER

32. (1) This Charter applies

(a) to the Parliament and government of Canada in respect of all matters within the authority of Parliament including all matters relating to the Yukon Territory and Northwest Territories; and

(b) to the legislature and government of each province in respect of all matters within the authority of the legislature of each province.

(2) Notwithstanding subsection (1), section 15 shall not have effect until three years after this section comes into force.

33.(1) Parliament or the legislature of a province may expressly declare in an Act of Parliament or of the legislature, as the case may be, that the Act or a provision thereof shall operate notwithstanding a provision included in section 2 or sections 7 to 15 of this Charter.

(2) An Act or a provision of an Act in respect of which a declaration made under this section is in effect shall have such operation as it would have but for the provision of this Charter referred to in the declaration.

(3) A declaration made under subsection (1) shall cease to have effect five years after it comes into force or on such earlier date as may be specified in the declaration.

(4) Parliament or a legislature of a province may re-enact a declaration made under subsection (1).

(5) Subsection (3) applies in respect of a re-enactment made under subsection (4).

CITATION

34. This part may be cited as the Canadian Charter of Rights and Freedoms.